Terror Crime Prevention with Communities

Terror Crime Prevention with Communities

Basia Spalek

Bloomsbury Academic
An imprint of Bloomsbury Publishing Plc

B L O O M S B U R Y
LONDON • NEW DELHI • NEW YORK • SYDNEY

Bloomsbury Academic

An imprint of Bloomsbury Publishing Plc

50 Bedford Square	1385 Broadway
London	New York
WC1B 3DP	NY 10018
UK	USA

www.bloomsbury.com

BLOOMSBURY and the Diana logo are trademarks of Bloomsbury Publishing Plc

First published 2013
Paperback edition first published 2015

© Basia Spalek, 2013

British Library Cataloguing-in-Publication Data
A catalogue record for this book is available from the British Library.

ISBN: HB:	978-1-8496-6481-3
PB:	978-1-4742-2367-6
ePDF:	978-1-8496-6484-4
ePub:	978-1-8496-6482-0

Library of Congress Cataloging-in-Publication Data
A catalog record for this book is available from the Library of Congress.

Typeset by Fakenham Prepress Solutions, Fakenham, Norfolk NR21 8NN

Contents

Acknowledgements

I wish to say thank you to Neil, my husband, simply for being there, for being part of the fabric of my everyday life, the presence that grounds me.

I wish to thank Laura Zahra McDonald, Zubeda Limbada, Raquel Beleza and Dan Silk for simply being ConnectJustice, and for being the great and inspiring friends that they are. (www.connectjustice.org)

I wish to thank Salwa El-Awa for our many colourful conversations and encounters, for her companionship and loyalty.

Finally, I wish to thank all those police officers, community members, officials, youth workers, young people and others who gave insights and access into their lives, without whom this book would not be possible.

Preface

Terror Crime Prevention with Communities is the result of over five years of amazing research collaborations, friendships and personal and professional growth. At the heart of this book there is an attempt to set out some key dynamics to what might be viewed as an ethical approach to doing counter-terrorism, whereby counter-terrorism is re-framed as conflict transformation. The book is part of a broader movement of researchers, practitioners, community members, policy officials, activists and others who believe that a better world is possible, that despite all the negativity that counter-terrorism has generated and continues to generate, it is possible for there to be ethical engagement and even partnerships between state and non-state actors for the purposes of ensuring the security of all. This thought brings me joy!

However, it is also with some sadness that I write this preface, for *Terror Crime Prevention with Communities* could well be my last academic book. In a world where policy makers are only interested in research that supports their particular perspectives, and where there are diminishing resources to conduct independent research, I have come to a position where I have asked myself how best can I use my time, my energy and my resources? It may be that new horizons beckon for me, that as I run along my journey of life new opportunities and challenges emerge. It is perhaps worth quoting from a book by Scott Jurek, an ultra-marathon legend, from whom I gather strength: 'No matter what you do, there are going to be haters out there. My Zen self tells me they're no worse than people who idolize you for the wrong reasons. What people think about you doesn't really matter. The trick is to be true to yourself' (Scott Jurek, with Steve Friedman, 2012: 160 *Eat & Run*, London: Bloomsbury).

Terror Crime Prevention with Communities: Trust, Community and Counter-Terrorism; an Introduction

Introduction

Terror Crime Prevention with Communities is the product of over 130 in-depth interviews which were carried out over five years, between 2007 and 2012, as part of a number of national and international research projects that I led. Interviews were conducted with community members, youth workers, police officers and other practitioners involved in counter-terrorism work, government and policy officials, and young people who might be 'at risk' of terrorism or terrorism-related offences. This book is also the product of international exchanges where counter-terrorism practice was discussed, involving academics, practitioners, Muslim community members and policy officials in a wide range of contexts, including Britain, the US, Northern Ireland, Egypt, Kyrgyzstan, Singapore, Moscow and Warsaw. I have also had many informal conversations with researchers, practitioners (including security service personnel) and government officials, and these too have helped to shape this book. An important element of the material presented here is the empirical data taken from interviews. Rarely do the voices of community members and junior practitioners feature in accounts of counter-terrorism. Analyses tend to be driven by theoretically sophisticated academic accounts which fail to grasp, or at least overlook, real-life experiences on the ground – for example, what it is like to be a young person experiencing counter-terrorism measures, what it is like to be a former politically motivated offender who is now working towards building peace within and between communities, or how a police officer goes about connecting with those communities deemed 'hard to reach' or deemed 'suspect' by the state. This book aims to address this deficit in knowledge by including, extensively, the voices of people experiencing, initiating and developing counter-terrorism measures.

It is important to highlight that whilst the predominant focus of the empirical data presented in this book is on responding to, and preventing, terrorism linked to Al Qaeda (AQ), the lessons learned and key messages from this work can be applied to other forms of terrorism, for example, those committed by far-right extremists, and can also be applied to tackling ideologically and politically motivated hate crimes. However, perhaps the specific significance and uniqueness of this book is that it stands in vast contrast to more dominant analyses of the kinds of threats that Britain faces from AQ-linked terrorism and what the social and political responses should be. After 9/11, and especially after the London bombings on 7 July 2005, a vast amount of literature was published regarding the nature of the threat posed to Britain and the West and what should be done about it. Examples include *Celsius 7/7: how the West's policy of appeasement has provoked yet more fundamentalist terror – and what has to be done now* by the current Education Secretary Michael Gove, *Londonistan: how Britain is creating a terror state within* by Daily Mail columnist Melanie Phillips, *While Europe Slept: how radical Islam is destroying the West from within* by Bruce Bawer, and *The Islamist* by Ed Husain. These books essentially have posed radical Islam as a potent threat to Britain and the West, not only in relation to terrorism but also a cultural and political threat to Western ideals of democracy and secularism. These books are an example of the kind of commonplace discourses that construct Islamic practices and beliefs as potentially dangerous and a potential barrier to social cohesion. These debates have deeper roots, and, according to Cesari (2005), Muslims' settlement in Europe and their claims for public recognition can be viewed as a threat by western secular states which separate politics from religion. Constructing Islamic identities and practices as 'radical' (which in some cases may be simply because individuals are religiously conservative and have a real or a perceived opposition to established secular values, see Spalek, Baker and Lambert, 2009) runs the risk that these are negatively labelled, attracting the attention of approaches to security that might be considered as requiring counter-insurgency and/or counter-subversion. The data presented in this book strongly challenge the idea that Britain and the West are under significant threat from 'radical Islam'. The data presented in *Terror Crime Prevention with Communities* illustrates that Muslims who might be perceived as 'radical' (whatever that term actually means) have worked hard to reduce the terrorist threat to Britain, in partnership with the police and other agencies. This book shows that portraying 'radical Muslims' as potential criminals or subversives is unjustifiable given that the data presented in the chapters that follow demonstrates that these individuals are potential allies and even partners for counter-terrorism as conflict transformation. Yet the portrayal of 'radical Islam' as a significant threat has captured the attention of successive governments. For example, in his foreword to the voluminous *Islamist Terrorism: the British Connections* (authored by Simcox, Stuart, Ahmed and Murray, 2011) Lord Carlile (who was an Independent Reviewer of Terrorist Legislation in Britain between 2001 and 2011 and provided Independent Oversight of the Prevent Strategy[1] in 2011) argues that the UK is something of a hub for the development of terrorists, and that 'Islamic extremism' remains the greatest and least-predictable threat. The question is why government policies have embraced so easily the construction of 'radical Islam' as a threat, so often ignoring empirical data around the contributions that many members of Muslim communities, including those that might be labelled as 'radical', have made, and continue to make, to Britain and the West. Perhaps this is an example of politicians adopting right-wing approaches that are seen as winning favour with majority public opinion as a way of gaining votes. Over many centuries there have been conflicts between Muslims and Christians, and portraying the supposed dangers of 'radical Islam' is an easy way of tapping into deep-seated fears that general populations have, not only in Britain but across the West, as a way of then implementing policies that politicians can argue make people safer, thus currying favour with Joe Public. At the same time, the rising presence of Muslim communities in the West, especially in Europe, taps into fears amongst general populations regarding migration, social cohesion and cultural identity. Perhaps creating a 'straw man' enemy in the form of 'radical Islam' is a useful mechanism through

---

[1] The counter-terrorism arena has expanded to include wide-ranging agencies beyond that of the police e.g. local councils, schools, universities and so forth through the Prevent aspect of the British counter-terrorism policy, CONTEST.

which to assuage people's worries about immigration; whilst there is little that politicians can do to stem the flow of migrants into the West, there are nevertheless severe counter-terrorism policies in place that can tackle the 'threat' from 'radical Islam'. *Terror Crime Prevention with Communities* therefore is a challenge to current strategic thinking around counter-terrorism, for this book does not portray 'radical Islam' as a threat, but rather draws on the experiences of Muslims (some of whom might be seen as 'radical' by some social and political commentators) and others to illustrate how ethically-driven counter-terrorism practices can be created and implemented.

This book also serves to highlight that, as a phenomenon, terrorism is a social process, not a concrete, single, event. *Terror Crime Prevention with Communities* invites its readers to view counter-terrorism also as a social process involving wide-ranging actors and institutions, and to analyse the wider social, political, emotional and cultural milieus doing counter-terrorism work. Across the world, separate from actors and institutions traditionally involved in counter-terrorism work – police officers, government officials, security services, judges – there are youth workers, educators, religious leaders, community members and organisations, including women's groups and others, who are involved in preventing extreme acts of violence through the youth work that they do, through challenging ideological extremisms that they encounter within their communities and through mentoring individuals deemed to be at risk of violent extremism. This heralds the development of what has been identified as 'community-based' approaches to counter-terrorism, involving considerable input from civil society. Counter-terrorism is therefore an arena that not only involves placing terrorist networks under surveillance and prosecuting them, but also involves engagement and partnerships between state actors (often police officers) and non-state actors (community members, religious and political leaders and so forth) to prevent acts of extreme violence. Security is implemented across wide-ranging actors and institutions. Involving a diverse set of state and non-state actors in the shared goal of preventing terrorism that is counter-terrorism work means the inclusion of different individuals and institutions with different priorities, and different ways of working. This is a complex task with competing narratives.

Terror Crime Prevention with Communities also invites its readers to view counter-terrorism as a form of conflict transformation, both positive and negative. This point links to ongoing debates about what terrorism actually is. Terrorism itself is a contested notion, so that terrorism should be approached as a concept and not as a label. As a concept, terrorism is a social construct, an idea, informing public opinions and perceptions which will impact on the conceptualisation and implementation of counter-terrorism strategies (Jackson, 2007). As a result, different actors and institutions will have different understandings of terrorism, and different viewpoints about how it should be prevented – thus, there will be points of divergence and contestation, alongside points of convergence. At the same time, implicit in many definitions of terrorism is the central theme of conflict, where conflict can mean struggle, incompatibility, collision, or disagreement. Thus, according to Wilkinson (2006: 6) 'terrorism is a weapon-system, which can be used by an enormous variety of groups and regimes with rapidly differing aims, ideologies and motivations'. According to the terminology used by the EU:

> terrorism is not an ideology but is a set of criminal tactics which deny the fundamental principles of democratic societies. Terrorist acts are those which aim to intimidate populations, compel states to comply with the perpetrators' demands, and/or destabilise or destroy the fundamental political, constitutional, economic or social structures of a country or an international organisation' (Europol TeSat, 2010: 5).

And according to Schmid (2004: 205–6) 'terrorism, by using violence against one victim, seeks to coerce and persuade others. The immediate victim is merely instrumental, the skin on a drum beaten to achieve a calculated impact on a wider audience'. The idea of conflict – that is, struggle, incompatibility, collision, or disagreement – is therefore implicit within many definitions of terrorism. Counter-terrorism can also involve conflict – struggle, incompatibility, collision, or disagreement – between different actors, institutions and nation-states, for if terrorism is a contested notion then doing counter-terrorism will also involve contestation. Ideas about what works, what approaches should be developed, who should be included, what the causes of terrorism are, are all unresolved questions. Different political, organisational and emotional cultures will impact upon counter-terrorism practices and so there are likely to be disagreements and incompatibilities over approaches.

Terror Crime Prevention with Communities further invites its readers to consider the ways in which seeming incompatibilities between wide-ranging actors and institutions can be overcome in order to do counter-terrorism work. This book can therefore be relevant to those who are engaged in contemporary approaches to peace-building. This is because much of the empirical data and analysis that is presented in this book is about how contexts (contexts here meaning the individual, group, community, organisation and state) characterised by conflict can undergo and experience change. Whilst there is an academically rich literature regarding models of counter-violent radicalisation, of peace building and conflict resolution (Lederach, 2010; Ramsbotham, Woodhouse and Miall, 2011), there is little on the actual lived experiences of those individuals and organisations involved in such initiatives. A key theme in this book is that by documenting and exploring the accounts of people involved in counter-terrorism as a form of conflict transformation we can learn more about the processes of dialogue, engagement, partnership, change and so forth. Here I would like to refer to the work of Victor Frankl, my inspiration for the significant use of individuals' accounts of their lived experiences in the research that I and my team have undertaken. Victor Frankl wrote a best-selling book based on his experiences of being a concentration camp survivor during World War Two called *Man's Search for Meaning*. At the start of this book, Frankl writes:

> This book does not claim to be an account of facts and events but of personal experiences, experiences which millions of prisoners have suffered time and again. It is the inside story of a concentration camp, told by one of its survivors. This tale is not concerned with the great horrors, which have already been described often enough (though less often believed), but with the multitude of small torments. In other words, it will try to answer this question: how was everyday life in a concentration camp reflected in the mind of the average prisoner? (Frankl, 1959, 3)

Victor Frankl's account of concentration-camp life is so compelling, providing details of the emotional and psychological states of the prisoners, precisely because it constitutes 'insider knowledge'. Frankl was a highly educated psychotherapist before he was transported to a concentration camp. He was therefore well placed to observe the emotional and psychological stresses being experienced by the prisoners, all the more so because he was experiencing similar impacts himself. Frankl's 'insider account' is particularly valuable because it is an 'ordinary' prisoner's account. In Frankl's own words:

this story is not about the suffering and death of great heroes or martyrs, nor is it about the prominent Capos – prisoners who acted as trusties, having special privileges – or well-known prisoners. Thus it is not so much concerned with the sufferings of the mighty, but with the sacrifices, the crucifixion and the deaths of the great army of unknown and unrecorded victims (Frankl, 1959: 3).

It is interesting that Victor Frankl refers to his book being about the experiences of 'ordinary prisoners', those not linked to wider power structures operating in the prison camps and in society at large where particular individuals' experiences can be lionised. Within the social sciences, the role that 'insider knowledge' might play in helping us to understand social problems has generated a large amount of discussion and debate. Wide-ranging theoretical and disciplinary positions such as anthropology, women's studies, critical race discourse, have, for a long time, challenged so-called 'neutral' research over the biases underpinning the objectivity that is claimed, presenting new insights that are underpinned by the experiences and perspectives of those whose lives are being studied. This has led to much discussion about what is meant by 'insider' knowledge. A large literature now posits that in reality researchers and research participants are both insiders and outsiders, occupying a multiplicity of subject positions (see Garland, Spalek and Chakraborti, 2006 for a discussion). This approach might be viewed as being linked to a 'postmodern paradigm' that has challenged the assumption within the social sciences that the proper end of social research is the production of objective knowledge (Lundy and McGovern, 2006). Whilst some academic disciplines have been significantly influenced by debates regarding what comprises knowledge, terrorism studies has for a long time consisted of 'outsider' knowledge claims made by institutions and actors that are directly linked to state-driven agendas. This is why critical terrorism studies emerged in the last decade or so, criticising traditional terrorism studies for being analytically and methodologically weak, relying too heavily on secondary information and for failing to understand terrorism, and counter-terrorism, through the perspectives and experiences of those experiencing state repression (Breen Smyth, 2007; Jackson, 2007). Counter-terrorism policy is an area dominated by geo-political power plays involving state and non-state actors, and 'insider knowledge' is rarely drawn upon when designing strategies, for research is dominated by state-centric perspectives founded on secondary sources and lacking the input of primary data collection and analysis (Breen Smyth: 2007; Jackson, 2007). There is therefore a danger that issues of security that matter at the individual and community level – including experiences of violence, inter- and intra-community tensions, social and economic exclusion, racism and so forth – are overlooked by the state-led focus upon the prevention of terrorism, both within the UK and overseas.

It also has to be said that the lack of empirical data is partly the result of over-theorisation within the social sciences, with there being generally a lack of interest in small-scale applied case studies. Rather than asking questions about how research results can be used in an applied context in order to help solve social problems like terrorism, reviewers, editors and those occupying positions of power in academia question the relevance of empirical data for broader theoretical questions. This results in research publications comprising over-theorised pieces, the practical and policy relevance of which is difficult to unpick. Moreover, it is difficult for social researchers to get work published in which empirical data actively questions taken-for-granted theoretical constructions because the review process will often err on the side of caution and uphold long-held theoretical stances. Thus, in relation to AQ-linked terrorism, whilst numerous publications have highlighted the 'war on terror' post 9/11 and the violation of human rights globally, few have addressed the question of whether it is possible to build trust between the state, security and police agencies and communities despite this broader context. Indeed, according to Eatwell and Goodwin (2010: 14), 'few studies bridge theoretical and empirical research on extremism with policy and practice'. Research should not be just about critiquing dominant political, social and economic structures, but rather, should provide possible solutions to the social issues confronting societies. For this to happen, it needs to be increasingly focussed upon local contexts and local solutions, with partnerships being built between researchers and local agencies and communities. Scholars working on questions of why some young British Muslims have committed terror acts are beginning to stress the need for specific research that looks at specific local contexts and their links to wider global geo-political dynamics. These researchers argue that it is important to focus upon British foreign policy and the social and economic reverberations of a colonial past, rather than focussing upon a socially constructed notion of 'new terrorism' that tends to view AQ related or linked attacks as part of some kind of global war against the West involving Islam (Githens-Mazer, 2010; Baker, 2010; Lambert, 2011).

Responding to, and preventing, terrorism tends to generate much discussion and writing about issues of spying upon communities, of infiltrating groups, of securitising and potentially criminalising members of those communities deemed as 'suspect' by state authorities. *Terror Crime Prevention with Communities*, whilst alluding to these issues, invites its readers to consider themes that link to how to go about doing ethically-driven counterterrorism practice. Ethically-driven counter-terrorism work, as highlighted in this book, involves the notions of credibility and connectivity for counterterrorism work, the role of community policing in counter-terrorism, trust and trust-building activities, engagement and partnerships between state and non-state actors, the role of emotions and questions of governance. These themes have been identified through the thematic analysis of the significant number of interviews that I and my research team have undertaken over the last five years. As such, a key strength of this book is that it is based upon many years of documenting the lived experiences and the perspectives of wide-ranging individuals. As *Terror Crime Prevention with Communities* sets out the multiple dynamics to counter-terrorism practice, conceptualising these within a broad understanding of what community-based approaches to counter-terrorism involve, this book should be of interest to people involved in peace-building and conflict-resolution activities, whether those activities are aimed at preventing or responding to terrorism or other forms of violence.

Terror Crime Prevention with Communities is comprised of eight chapters. Chapter 2 focuses on the importance of credibility when thinking about counter-terrorism as conflict transformation. The chapter highlights that the notion of credibility is so important for understanding counter-terrorism practice because counter-terrorism is about responding to, and working within, conflict. For example, post 9/11 there are deep contestations regarding 'truth', with the wide interest in conspiracy theories being just one example of the contested knowledge here. As with wars and other conflicts there are, post 9/11, multiple truths and a generallack of effort to find a unique (which the world majority would agree on) common understanding. Chapter 2 sets out some of the dynamics to the struggles, incompatibilities and disagreements in relation to responses to terrorism linked to or influenced by Al

Qaeda (AQ) since 9/11. In particular, the US-led 'war on terror' post 9/11, 'new terrorism' discourse, the securitisation of Muslim communities, and the ongoing debates around citizenship, Muslim identities and loyalties are highlighted as examples of significant conflict underpinning responses to AQ-linked terrorism. Questions are then raised about how individuals – whether police officers or other practitioners or community members – build relationships and linkages for the purposes of counter-terrorism within such a challenging environment? A key theme is credibility; credibility allows us to think about counter-terrorism practice as going beyond merely responding to terrorism and about implementing practice that comprises real engagement. Credibility is such an important aspect to counter-terrorism, for this is an arena rife with conflicting viewpoints and experiences, with rumours and obscurity. Therefore, when challenging terrorist ideologies, when working with vulnerable people, when explaining to communities the tactics of the police in relation to specific operations, it is important for the individuals involved to have built credibility with their target audiences.

Chapter 2 highlights that 'doing credibility' is about individuals using their positionalities when engaging with others in order to build individuals' trust and respect. The notion of positionality features significantly in social science research, and involves the acknowledgement that individuals comprise multiple identities, multiple identity positions, in relation to the social categories of 'race'/ethnicity, faith, gender, class, sexuality and so forth. At any one time an individual therefore has a range of positionalities which will be drawn upon in diverse ways depending on the wider social context and the factors inherent within a specific encounter. At the same time, these position-alities will interact with each other in complex ways, referred to in the social science literature as intersectionalities. Intersectionalities therefore refer to the linkages between 'race'/ethnicity, faith, gender, class, sexuality etc. and how these linkages themselves influence and are influenced by the separate and diverse positionalities that a person has. Thus, an individual will have a complex, constantly moving, set of positionalities and intersectionalities which will influence, as well as be influenced by, their social encounters and experiences. The research that I and my team have been undertaking would seem to suggest the key role that positionalities and intersectionalities play in conflict transformation for a diverse range of actors, including young people, youth workers, police officers, probation officers, community members and others. The research suggests that positionalities are drawn upon in multiple and complex ways in order to build new connections within and between communities for the purposes of preventing and responding to terrorism. This allows the development of dialogue, engagement and partnerships to take place in relation to countering terrorism. The transformative nature of this process highlights new possibilities – contexts characterised by fear or mistrust or violent action can undergo significant change suggesting that struggles, disagreements and incompatibilities within and between communities and between individuals can be deconstructed, a form of conflict resolution. Chapter 2 also suggests that credibility is about maintaining a position that seeks to achieve social justice within an unjust world. This may mean challenging structures of dominance and power, and so individuals may be involved in deconstructing power relations that victimise the powerless. As a result, credible individuals run the risk of being labelled subversives by dominant power elites. Individuals also run the risk of losing their credibility if they are seen to be engaging with actors who are perceived to be against the interests of those whose trust they have gained. Credibility is also about being embedded within communities and within networks. It is about ongoing engagement and relationship building, and about being available at short notice to de-fuse difficult situations. This can also include individuals understanding 'the street', street-based culture and how this links to vulnerabilities to terrorism. Credibility also involves leadership, being able to implement creative initiatives which challenge those vulnerable to extreme violence.

Chapter 3 takes a close look at police and community engagement in relation to counter terrorism as conflict transformation. Strikingly absent from peace-building and conflict resolution research material are in-depth analyses of the interactions between police and communities. Police–community relations are an important dynamic of any peace-building and/or conflict resolution activities, for there are often tensions between police and communities during conflict. Experiences and perceptions of inequality within societies are often related to a lack of protection within existing frameworks of the law, and the disproportionate use of state power against victimised or suspect communities often employing militarised forms of policing. Even within societies characterised as comprisingpeaceful liberal democracies, there are often significant tensions and conflicts between police and particular communities, with police being accused of racism, Islamophobia, of colonial practices, of sexist and gendered stereotypical assumptions and so forth. There is, therefore, great importance in focussing upon police and community dynamics within wide-ranging societies, whether those societies are in conflict, post conflict or 'at peace'. In relation to counter terrorism as conflict transformation, my research team and I have undertaken a number of studies examining police and community engagement and partnership work. This has generated much insight into issues affecting and influencing police and community relations and how trust can be built between police officers and community members, despite wider political, cultural, social and other tensions. Chapter 3 therefore highlights some of the key issues emanating from a focus upon police and community interactions, with quotations from police officers and community members about their experiences. It is important to highlight that there are multiple positionalities that police officers and community members hold, and so there is an extremely diverse set of experiences and perceptions when thinking about policing. This is important to note, because for too long police and communities have been viewed as overarching categories of people who are diametrically opposed to each other. The research presented in chapter 3 demonstrates that police officers also are members of communities and that communities include individuals whose jobs are in policing. This provides added complexities to thinking about counter terrorism practice.

Chapter 3 also looks at the role of community policing and the challenges here when thinking about responding to terrorism as conflict transformation. Much has been written about community policing, and a significant literature now exists in relation to community policing and counter-terrorism. The research presented in chapter 3 stresses that there seems to be a real mistrust amongst young people towards police officers and so it is crucial for police to work with and engage people from within communities who can reach out to young people. The importance of police and communities engaging with each other outside a crisis event is also highlighted, as this can serve to humanise police and community relations. It is important, though, to highlight that there can be major differences in perceptions between police officers and communities. Thus, police officers may express the need for a covert style of counter-terrorism policing, and believe that communities cannot expect 'hard' policing tactics to be removed for the sake of relationship-building, even though communities argue that they dislike the use of tactics like surveillance, stop-and-search and informant-based approaches. It is also important to consider that police officers feel unsafe walking in certain neighbourhoods or areas and ask what responsibility community members have to ensure the safety of officers?

Chapter 4 examines citizenship, responsibilisation and trust in relation to understanding counter-terrorism as conflict transformation. In many countries across the world, including Britain, the US, Canada and Australia, counter-terrorism policy includes a large focus upon active citizenship. Individuals as citizens are expected to act responsibly in the face of threats from terrorism, spotting signs of vulnerability within their family, work and other cohorts, and informing appropriate authorities. As in other areas of social policy – crime, health, welfare – individuals are being viewed as an important resource for preventing terrorism, through their responsibilities as active citizens and as members of wider communities. This focus on active citizenship within counter-terrorism policy constitutes a radical shift from traditional counter-terrorism policies and practices. States are attempting to engage, and even to build partnerships, with individual citizens and with the wider communities to which they belong, rather than automatically drawing upon 'hard' counter-terrorism tactics that involve the use of informants, surveillance and so forth. However, chapter 4 highlights how, in the context of security, there are many historical and contemporary examples of individual citizens, and their communities, experiencing differentiated state-led approaches.

The chapter then examines how states can encourage and actively persuade citizens to work within state-driven counter-terrorism agendas, in a context of differentiated citizenship, where there may be competing loyalties associated with experiences of belonging at a global, as well as national and local level. In the post 9/11 context, for example, what challenges are there for policy makers attempting to involve and engage with members of Muslim communities for counter-terrorism purposes? A key theme presented in chapter 4 is that of trust. Interviews with police officers, probation officers, youth workers, community members and others indicate the importance of trust for 'softer' counter-terrorism policies. It seems that trust enables state and non-state actors to negotiate spaces of engagement and even partnership within the complex counter-terrorism terrain. This suggests that underpinning 'softer' counter-terrorism policies and practices are themes that resonate more directly with conflict transformation – the ability of state and non-state actors to work through any incompatibilities and struggles they may have, with trust serving as the social glue for this.

Chapter 5 examines engagement and partnership as key notions for under-standing counter-terrorism work as conflict transformation. Engagement might be thought of as the building of relationships between actors through a process of interaction which includes ongoing dialogue and debate, the ability to listen to the experiences and perspectives of the person with whom one is engaging, and can include more informal socialising such as attending weddings or funerals or other significant occasions. Ongoing positive engagement can lead to the establishment of mutually beneficial, equality-based working partnerships, in which the trust and commitment develop for individuals/organisations to be able to co-operate for the purposes of counter-terrorism. In these cases, initial face-to-face contact can develop into relationships that involve police officers working with community members on a host of areas related to counter-terrorism, from issues in relation to community safety and cohesion, to work with young people and direct challenges to violent extremist propaganda and structures. Chapter 5 raises the question of whether engagement and partnership, when applied to counter-terrorism, is one-sided, in that it is communities that are expected to engage with state actors like the police, and to partner them, on terms that have already been set by government and/or state-led agendas. Given that increasingly, policing is viewed as an activity that involves not only policing agencies, but also other statutory agencies and, crucially, communities, what opportunities and challenges are there for engagement and partnerships? Might these be important mechanisms through which to enhance democratic policing that pays due regard to human rights issues, and the fostering of community well-being? The chapter highlights that whilst engagement and partnership can be carefully constructed with particular community members, it is key not to overlook the importance of police officers engaging with communities more generally; engagement and partnership can have different meanings and involve different approaches to enhancing the quality of life for communities, building inclusivity, developing connections with women, building relationships, engaging with wider political issues, moving at the community's pace, respect and understanding. There can be tensions between 'hard-ended' intelligence-led approaches to counter-terrorism, in which community engagement and partnership are not priorities, and 'softer' community-focused approaches that are about relationship-building. Information sharing is a key issue for engagement and partnerships.

Chapter 6 looks at the role of emotions in relation to counter-terrorism as conflict transformation. It is argued that whilst some research has examined the emotional impacts of counter-terrorism measures on targeted communities (Spalek et al., 2009), rarely have emotions been explored in relation to any engagement and partnerships that may take place between state and non-state actors. Chapter 6 demonstrates that such engagements do involve emotional dynamics. Moreover, citizenship is experienced not only legally, politically and socially, but also at a profoundly emotional level. Essentially, counter-terrorism is a field of policy and practice rife with emotions. Being aware of emotions, being able to negotiate them, being able to draw on them constructively rather than destructively: these are strategies that practitioners, community members and policy makers should understand and be able to use in order to create opportunities for effective work. Chapter 6 focuses on providing some exploration and analysis of the role of emotions in counter-terrorism, explaining why they should be of concern to practitioners, community members, policy makers and others who work in counter-terrorism. Data from interviews with community members and police officers is presented in order to illustrate the emotional aspects of counter-terrorism. This makes it clear that destructive emotions can be generated by terrorism and counter-terrorism, but that nonetheless, community members and police practitioners can understand these emotional dynamics in order to reduce the harms caused by negative emotions. Community members and police officers can also work towards creating opportunities for the expression of constructive emotions.

'Emotional intelligence' is a theme that is also discussed in this chapter. What does it mean to be emotionally intelligent and why should this matter to practitioners, community members and policy makers when thinking about counter-terrorism as conflict transformation? The notion of healing is also addressed; this rarely features in the conflict resolution literature. It seems that rather than healing, peace is a concept that is discussed. Thus, a distinction has been drawn between positive and negative peace. Negative peace relates to the cessation of direct violence, whilst positive peace can be understood as the dismantling of structural and cultural violence (Ramsbotham, Woodhouse and Miall, 2011). Both negative and positive peace can be at the level of the individual, the family, the community or at the international level. Negative peace can co-exist with repression, injustice and exploitation, whilst positive peace relates to the structural and cultural order as being legitimate and just. Of course, the difficulty with the concept of positive peace is that there may be different perceptions anad experiences of justice and legitimacy, so that one group may feel that it is experiencing positive peace while another group may not see it so (Ramsbotham, Woodhouse and Miall, 2011). Interestingly, within conflict resolution literature peace is discussed and analysed, but the related concept of healing rarely features. Healing is a more interesting notion because this refers to the processes of change at individual, community, societal and international levels. Whereas peace suggests an end-goal, healing is suggestive of continuity, of a continual process – for what is the end result of healing and how do we know we have been healed? In relation to conflict, the notion of peace is more problematic than healing because often conflicts lead to substantial traumas, and trauma creates its own conflict, whether at the level of the individual, community, society or internationally. So whilst trauma can undergo healing, it is unclear whether that healing has an endpoint, whereas the notion of peace is more suggestive of an end point. Healing also encapsulates the role of emotional, psychological, cultural and structural processes. Yet the role of emotions and emotional intelligence in conflict transformation is rarely given a significant amount of research and policy attention.

Chapter 6 also suggests that individuals and communities may share emotions, which underpin their shared meanings (Moisi, 2009). Struggles take place globally over the emotional-political landscapes of communities, so that 'winning hearts and minds' is a strategy adopted by terrorists. Equally, counter-terrorism is increasingly attempting to win 'hearts and minds' through helping to empower communities in relation to politics, religiosity, social and economic deprivation and so forth. If individuals linked to, or influenced by,

AQ networks draw upon their emotional intelligence to influence individuals emotionally and thus encourage engagement in extremist activities, reasoning alone will not be a response sufficient to prevent terrorism: rather, practitioners working in this area need to be emotionally intelligent and be able to empathise and make those deemed at risk feel comfortable with them in order to allow for effective prevention work to take place. This reflects current thinking within cognitive psychology, which views emotions as being intertwined with human thinking and behaviour. Therefore, it might be suggested that a way of altering cognitions and transforming how individuals relate to, and interact with, the world is through an awareness of, and working with, emotions. So whilst the notion of peace in the conflict resolution literature refers to the abolition of structural, cultural and direct violence, it is argued in chapter 6 that the notion of peace should also encapsulate the process of healing, which invites a focus on, and consideration of, emotions, at the individual, community, nation state and international levels.

Chapter 7 explores some issues around questions of governance and community-based approaches to counter-terrorism. This chapter highlights that the 'War on Terror' associated with AQ-linked 'new terrorism' uses a set of rationalities and technologies which are top-down, comprised of international and national state policies instigated and influenced by elite political, social, media and other groupings. Nonetheless, 'bottom-up' approaches that are community-based can challenge 'top-down' approaches. 'Bottom-up' approaches that stress liberal freedoms can involve working with individuals and groups deemed 'dangerous' by 'top-down' approaches. 'Bottom-up' approaches involve community members and potentially bring greater public scrutiny of counter-terrorism. However, as this chapter also demonstrates, the involvement of community members in engagement and oversight of counter-terrorism can be challenging. The chapter highlights that there can be tensions between approaches to counter-terrorism that stress community cohesion and those approaches that stress liberal freedoms associated with democracy. The chapter points to an unresolved question for many counter-terrorism practitioners, for policy makers, for researchers and for community members: within a society, where should the balance lie between the embracing of ethical freedoms in relation to 'extreme' identities, and the governance of identity? Extreme or radical identifications are not necessarily problematic but violent actions associated with them are. Therefore, can there be alternative forms of agency that allow for the expression of radical or extreme identities which are democratic and do not involve violence?

Finally, in the conclusion the various themes identified and discussed within each chapter are put together. The conclusion highlights how the ideas and reflections presented in this book are relevant for a wide range of social issues and contexts, relevant for not only counter-terrorism but also for peace-building and conflict resolution arenas. The conlusion ends by highlighting that *Terror Crime Prevention with Communities* bears testimony to the many practitioners, community members, policy officials and researchers who have shown significant leadership and courage in implementing ethically-driven initiatives aimed at preventing terrorism.

Conclusion

Terror Crime Prevention with Communities is an important book for understanding counter-terrorism practice. *Terror Crime Prevention with Communities* also raises a number of key themes that are relevant for peace-building and conflict-resolution initiatives and programmes. It is essential to stress the importance of drawing heavily upon the voices of individuals – be they young people, practitioners or community members – for their experiences and viewpoints. This is because it is at this level, the level of human experience and perception, that new learning takes place and so researchers can draw on this in order to help shape policies and practices. We have many theoretical models in the fields of counter-terrorism, counter violent radicalisation, peace-building and conflict resolution. What we need now is a much greater emphasis on understanding, truly understanding, people's experiences and perceptions to create fresh ways of thinking about wide-ranging social issues, including counter-terrorism. With this in mind, we now turn to Chapter 2, which explores the notion of credibility for doing counter-terrorism work.

Bibliography

Baker, A. (2010) *Extremists in Our Midst: Confronting Terror*. Hampshire: Palgrave.

Bawer, B. (2006) *While Europe Slept: How Radical Islam is Destroying the West From Within*. New York: Random House.

Breen Smyth, M. (2007) 'A Critical Research Agenda For The Study Of Political Terror'. *European Political Science*, Vol. 6, pp. 260–7.

Cesari, J. (2005) *European Muslims and the Secular State*. London: Ashgate Publishing.

Eatwell, R. and Goodwin, M. (2010) 'Introduction' in: R. Eatwell and M. Goodwin (eds) *The New Extremism in Twenty-First-Century Britain*. London: Routledge 1–20.

Europol TeSat (2010) 'EU Terrorism Situation and Trend Report', www.consilium. europa.eu/uedocs/cmsUpload/TE-SAT%202010.pdf (accessed 4 December 2011).

Frankl, V. (1959) *Man's Search for Meaning*. London: Rider.

Garland, J., Spalek, B. and Chakraborti, N. (2006) 'Hearing Lost Voices: Issues in Researching Hidden Minority Ethnic Communities'. *The British Journal of Criminology*, Vol. 46, pp. 423–37.

Githens-Mazer, J. (2010) 'Moblization, recruitment, violence and the street' in: R. Eatwell and M. Goodwin (eds) *The "New" Extremism in Twenty-First-Century Britain*. London: Taylor & Francis, pp. 47–66.

Gove, M. (2006) *Celsius 7/7: How the West's Policy of Appeasement Has Provoked Yet More Fundamentalist Terror – and What Has to be Done Now*. London: Weidenfeld & Nicolson.

Husain, E. (2007) *The Islamist: why I joined Radical Islam in Britain*. London: Penguin.

Jackson, R. (2007) 'The core commitments of critical terrorism studies'. *European Political Science*, 6, pp. 244–51.

Lambert, R. (2011) *Countering Al-Qaeda in London: Police and Muslims in Partnership*. London: Hurst.

Lederach, J. (2010) *Building Peace: Sustainable Reconciliation in Divided Societies*. Second edition, Washington: US Institute of Peace Press.

Lundy, P. and McGovern, M. (2006) 'Participation, Truth and Partiality: participatory action research, community-based truth-telling and post-conflict transition in Northern Ireland'. *Sociology* 40 (1), pp. 71–88.

Moisi, D. (2009) *The Geopolitics of Emotion: How Cultures of Fear, Humiliation, and Hope are Reshaping the World*. New York: Anchor Books.

Phillips, M. (2006) *Londonistan: how Britain is Creating a Terror State Within*, London: Gibson Square.

Ramsbotham, O., Woodhouse, T. and Miall, H. (2011) *Contemporary Conflict Transformation*. 3rd edition, Cambridge: Polity Press.

Simcox, R., Stuart, H., Ahmed, H. and Murray, D. (2011) *Islamist Terrorism: the British Connections*. London: The Henry Jackson Society.

Spalek, B., Lambert, R. and Baker, A. H. (2009) 'Minority Muslim communities and criminal justice: stigmatized UK faith identities post 9/11 and 7/7', in H. S. Bhui (ed.), *Race and Criminal Justice*. London: Sage, pp. 170–87.

2

Credibility in Counter-Terrorism Practice

Introduction

A key characteristic of today's information-based society is that people no longer automatically believe mainstream, dominant, accounts of events. People are increasingly cynical about information that governing elites produce, and they do not necessarily accept 'expert' opinion or advice. Counter-terrorism is just like any other social policy area – whilst ruling elites are concerned to instigate a series of programmes and initiatives aimed at what they believe reduces a society's risks of terrorism, these are often critiqued and questioned by citizens. Post-9/11 conspiracy theories have proliferated and have been circulated in online communities, focussing on questions like: why did the world's most powerful air force fail to intercept any of the four hijacked planes? why did the Twin Towers collapse so quickly, within their own footprint, after fires on a few floors that lasted only for an hour or two? how could a skyscraper, which was not hit by a plane, collapse so quickly and symmetrically, when no other steel-framed skyscraper has collapsed because of fire? (*BBC News Magazine*, 2011). A number of surveys suggest that many people are cynical about the mainstream accounts of the causes of the attacks in the US on the World Trade Center and other targets. For example, according to a BBC poll carried out for the BBC2 programme *The Conspiracy Files*, a quarter of young Britons believe that the attacks were carried out by the government of the United States (BBC2, 2006).

Clearly, there are struggles, disagreements and incompatibilities within and between individuals, groups, communities and states concerning accounts of the causes of 9/11 and, consequently, what the solutions should be. In particular, the US-led 'war on terror', 'new terrorism' discourse, the securitisation of Muslim communities, and the ongoing debates around citizenship, Muslim identities and loyalties are examples of areas that have generated significant debate and controversy in relation to state responses to terrorism linked to Al Qaeda (AQ) post 9/11. This raises the question of how it is that individuals – whether as police officers or other practitioners or community members – build relationships and networks with each other for the purposes of 'counter-terrorism' within such a challenging environment. Moreover, when considering young people who might be at risk of violent radicalisation, whose voices do they listen to? If young people are accessing jihadist material available on the internet alongside other media, and if they are seeing the double standards that foreign policy often raises in terms of responses associated with the 'war on terror' and the violation of human rights and international law, how is it possible to deter young people from committing acts of violence themselves?

This chapter highlights the importance of the notion of credibility for counter-terrorism practice. Where there are multiple perspectives and multiple truths, credibility ensures that the credible person's message is at least listened to if not wholly adopted. There are perhaps different degrees of credibility, influencing the extent to which a person is convincing, believable or worthy of belief. Credibility is such an important aspect of counter-terrorism because this is an arena rife with conflicting viewpoints and experiences, with rumours and obscurity. Therefore, when challenging terrorist ideologies, when working with vulnerable people, when explaining police tactics in relation to specific operations taking place within communities, it is important for the individuals involved to have built credibility with their target audiences. This chapter demonstrates that credibility often involves drawing upon and using one's positionalities – one's faith, gender, ethnicity, political affiliations etc. – when engaging with others in order to gain their trust and their respect. Credibility is also about maintaining a position that seeks to achieve social justice within an unjust world. This may mean challenging structures of dominance and power, and so individuals may be involved in deconstructing power relations that victimise the powerless. As a result, credible individuals run the risk of being labelled subversives by dominant power elites. They also run the risk of losing their credibility if they are seen to be engaging with actors who are perceived to be against the interests of those whose trust they have gained. For example, youth workers may run the risk of losing credibility with the young people that they work with if they are perceived as being too closely linked with the police. Credibility also involves individuals being embedded within communities and within networks, therefore it is about ongoing engagement and relationship building. It is also about being available at short notice to defuse difficult situations. Credibility is therefore about grassroots-level engagement and relationship-building, and this may involve an understanding of 'the street', of street-based culture and linkages with vulnerabilities to terrorism alongside other forms of violence. Credibility is also about understanding the many social, cultural and political factors that shape individuals' lives and working towards supporting individuals who are vulnerable to committing, and being the targets of, acts of violence. Credibility can also involve leadership. This means having the ability to question assumptions and practices, having the ability to create new frameworks of understanding for policy and practice, and the ability to challenge target audiences so that this challenge translates into actual behavioural change.

The importance of credibility can be easily overlooked for this can raise uncomfortable issues for policy makers, particularly those who see radicalism of any kind as a threat to liberal democracy.[1] Credible individuals who oppose social injustice may be viewed as a threat by governing elites since these individuals do not fit in easily with state-led agendas that often place the security and needs of the nation-state over and above wider issues of social justice. Indeed, credible people may be classified as 'dissenters', individuals who 'cause trouble' for the authorities because they are agents of social and political change (Hewitt, Spalek and McDonald, 2012). Hence embracing the notion of credibility at the core of counter-terrorism practice is problematic and not without challenges. Although there is an increasing acknowledgement in policy-making circles that state-led approaches will not reach those audiences most susceptible to terrorists' messages, there is a lack of appreciation of the importance of credibility, what this means and how this might be used in counter-terrorism. This chapter highlights that in order to

---

[1] See the Prevent Review 2011 where there is a clear, and potentially contradictory, message: that government will not fund, or work with, extremist groups, where extremism is understood as meaning to be in active opposition to fundamental British values, including democracy, the rule of law, individual liberty and the mutual respect and tolerance of different faiths and beliefs.

reach out to people and to provide them with non-violent alternatives it is important to have credibility with them. Post 9/11 there are deep contestations regarding 'truth', with the wide interest in conspiracy theories being just one example of contested knowledge. As with wars and other conflicts there are, post 9/11, multiple truths, and a general lack of effort to find a unique (which the world majority would agree on) common understanding. As there is such disagreement over the causes of 9/11 and the responses to it, it is important for credible members of communities to draw on their positionalities in order to provide credible responses to terrorism. Where there are multiple perspectives and multiple truths, credibility ensures that the credible person's message is at least listened to.

Counter-terrorism as conflict

The 'war on terror'

The post 9/11 era is clearly one of conflict. From the very initial inception of the US led response to AQ linked terrorism, the language of war has been used, as well as orientalist discourse regarding the threat of Muslims to western values. In the aftermath of 9/11, the USA declared a 'war on terror', which was very much shaped by President George Bush's political discourse against 'those who envy Western values and Western freedom'.[2] By taking this stand, not only did President Bush offend the feelings of the Muslim populations around the world, he also recalled the history of some of the worst conflicts between the Christian and Muslim worlds through reference to the Crusades.[3] This notion was thus seen as an attack on Muslims whose faith is often viewed as defining freedom differently from the western world, yet who do not necessarily 'envy' the West for its 'values'. Many Muslims across the globe have not yet forgotten the history of centuries of western colonialism

---

[2] Bush's public speeches immediately following the 9/11 attacks e.g. Bush, George W. "Remarks upon arrival at the White House," 16 September 2001, White House News Releases, http://www.whitehouse. gov/news/releases/2001/09/20010916-2.html [19/12/08] and "President Bush, Colombia President Uribe Discuss Terrorism," 25 September 2002, White House News Releases, http://www.white-house.gov/news/releases/2002/09/20020925-1.html [19/12/08]

[3] Bush, George W. "Remarks upon arrival at the White House," 16 September 2001, White House News Releases, http://www.whitehouse.gov/news/releases/2001/09/20010916-2.html# [19/12/08]

and exploitation and, as a consequence think of the Crusades as a series of wars proving the Western/Christian ambition to control Muslim lands. By framing the response to 9/11 as a 'crusade' and a 'war on terror', alongside the launch of attacks on Afghanistan and Iraq, President Bush elicited strong popular and intellectual reactions across the Muslim world.[4] Specifically, Bush's remarks provoked animosity towards what has been perceived as a new colonialist era echoing the historic exploitation of resources of the developing countries by Western/Christian civilisations.

'New terrorism'

Alongside the 'war on terror', the notion of 'new terrorism' has entered into public discourse, used by security experts and government officials, whereby 'Islamist' terrorism has been declared an unprecedented and unpredictable global danger. 'Islamists' are also viewed as a danger to liberal democracy. As an example of this, the following is a quotation taken from the British Government's Prevent strand of its main counter-terrorism policy:

> Islamist extremists can specifically attack the principles of participation and cohesion, rejection of which we judge to be associated with an increased willingness to use violence. (Home Office, 2011, 20); Prevent Review:

'New terrorism' discourse has greatly contributed to the construction of Muslim minorities as 'suspect', necessitating their surveillance and control by the state (Mythen and Walklate 2006; Poynting and Mason 2008; Spalek and McDonald 2010). A number of researchers have argued that in the context of 'new terrorism', Muslim communities have become the new 'suspect communities' (Spalek, El-Awa and McDonald, 2009; Pantazis and Pemberton, 2009; Hickman and Silvestri, 2011; Choudhury and Fenwick, 2011). In a recent report by the Equality and Human Rights Commission in the UK, into the impact of counter-terrorism legislation on Muslim communities, it was highlighted that:

---

[4] E.g. 'More than ⅓ of US Muslims see War on Islam', *Washington Times*, 19 October 2004 http://www.washingtontimes.com/news/2004/oct/19/20041019-115241-3792r/ [19/12/08] and Evans, 'War on Terrorism Looks Too Much Like a War on Islam, Arab Scholar Warns' 27 January 2003 UCLA International Institute http://www.international.ucla.edu/article.asp?parentid=3010

When it comes to experiences of counter-terrorism, Muslims and non-Muslims from the same local areas who participated in this research appear to live 'parallel lives'. Counter-terrorism measures are contributing to a wider sense among Muslims that they are being treated as a 'suspect community' and targeted by authorities simply because of their religion. Many participants, while not referring to specific laws or policies, felt that counter-terrorism law and policy generally was contributing towards hostility to Muslims by treating Muslims as a 'suspect group', and creating a climate of fear and suspicion towards them (Choudhury and Fenwick, 2001: v).

The breadth and depth of wide-ranging new laws and state powers in relation to the perceived threat from 'new terrorism' have the potential to criminalise vast sections of Muslim communities, a fact which has been highlighted (McGovern, 2010). In Britain, powers and policies that have been particularly criticised include the Terrorism Act (2006), which extended the power to detain suspects without charge from 7 to 28 days because of the supposedly qualitatively different threat now posed; the use of the asylum system to detain Muslim foreign nationals and the extended powers of the Special Immigration Appeals Commission (SIAC) by the Anti-Terrorism Crime and Security Act (2001) (McGovern, 2010); the recently rescinded power to designate places where people can be stopped and searched without reasonable grounds for suspicion under Section 44; stops and searches under Schedule 7; and the use of 'extraordinary rendition' with allegations of torture having taken place in detention facilities in Afghanistan and Guantanamo Bay. Section 44 of the Terrorism Act 2000 allowing stop and search without suspicion was overturned by the Home Secretary in July 2010 following a refusal of an appeal by the Home Office to the European Courts of Human Rights against an earlier decision that had found Section 44 to be illegal. In 2010 the Home Secretary announced that a rapid review of key counter-terrorism and security powers was underway. The review looked at which counter-terrorism powers and measures could be rolled back in order to restore the balance between civil liberties and counter-terrorism powers. Control orders and stop and search powers were two of the key issues under review. In January 2012 control orders were replaced by Terrorism Prevention and Investigation Measures (T-Pims), which have fewer controls but greater surveillance. Control orders have been heavily criticised by civil liberties groups for their severe restrictions of individuals who have not been charged with any offences. Control orders came under attack from within the Coalition government, leading to the change. Wide-ranging new counter-terrorism laws have also been implemented across the European Union, the US, Australia and other countries, leading to accusations that they are trying to normalise 'the exception' by establishing an apparent permanent emergency.

Within liberal democratic systems, sovereign power derives from the people (through elections) and is exercised on their behalf by the government, which is held accountable via legal frameworks and laws. 9/11 and its aftermath has impacted upon the operation of sovereignty at the individual (citizen identity) and the collective (state identity) level. It is Muslim communities, as the source of terror threats from the 'inside' (home-grown terrorism) and the 'outside' (from international networks and patterns of identity formations that transcend nation-state boundaries), whose identities have been securitised and deemed 'a threat'. Securitisation is the instigation of emergency politics whereby a particular social issue that becomes securitised is responded to above and beyond established rules and frameworks that exist within what might be termed 'normal politics' (Jutila, 2006).

The breadth and remit of some of the counter-terrorism measures in the UK have generated considerable controversy. Whilst the dominant policy rhetoric may be that communities can be engaged and partnered in countering terrorism, in reality there is substantial journalistic and other commentary about the extensive 'use' of informants by the police and security services (Kundnani, 2009). The lack of clarity over, and considerable debate regarding, the question of who is my enemy has contributed to a situation where some Muslims, who have partnered police agencies for counter-terrorism purposes, have found themselves simultaneously monitored by security and other agencies, and viewed as potential 'dangerous others' (Silk, O'Rawe and Spalek, 2013). Thus in a recent research report by Spalek and McDonald (2011), examining police and community engagement post 9/11, it was highlighted that:

> In areas deemed at 'high risk' of violent extremism – by the authorities or communities – it is likely that both overt and covert policing is taking place. This creates a tension and challenge for community members who may be engaging with overt police officers whilst also believing that they are the

subject of covert observation and other operations. (Spalek and McDonald,
2011: 6).

Muslim community members have been approached by the security services in
order to act as informants. This has helped create a sense of grievance amongst
many Muslims, with individuals arguing that they feel they are members of
a suspect community. Individuals have spoken about the consequences of
being viewed with suspicion on their life and the lives of their family, which
can result in job losses, family breakdown and ostracisation from their wider
communities. Individuals have also described how those people considered
by the authorities as suspicious are often too frightened to report incidents
of being stopped and questioned – even to supportive community groups
(Spalek, El-Awa and McDonald, 2009). So whilst the notion that 'communities
can defeat terrorism' has become a common mantra, creating some interesting
engagement and partnership work between communities and the police
(which will be discussed further in Chapters 3, 4 and 5), there is ongoing
tension between community-focussed approaches and those community-
targeted approaches that have been highlighted above. The question is where
should the balance lie between community-targeted and community-focussed
approaches within a liberal democratic society?

Post-9/11 conflict over values has also entered the counter-terrorism arena.
Since 9/11 there has been significant debate about the seeming incompatibility of Muslim populations in traditionally Judeo-Christian and also, more
recently, secular populations in Europe. Muslims' loyalties and their citizenship
have been scrutinised and questions have been raised about the compatibility
of Muslim communities' values with those of liberal democracy. Numerous
surveys have been undertaken nationally and internationally, comparing
and contrasting the views of Muslims with those of non-Muslims, as well as
trying to understand Muslim citizens' views on Sharia law, Islamic or Muslim
identities, Islamophobia, Muslims' trust in policing and so forth. Professor
Clive Field wrote an interesting article in 2011 which explored themes of
incompatibility or disagreement between British Muslims and 'Britishness' by
studying data from 25 national survey polls in Britain relating to the views of
young (under-35) British Muslims. For Field (2011), a clear majority of young
Muslim Britons, ranging from just over half to four-fifths according to the

topic concerned and the survey, are 'moderate' and 'mainstream'. For Field this means that they are actively committed to their faith, uphold principles of Sharia, and are generally satisfied with Britain although they feel vulnerable due to worsening Islamophobia. Field (2011) also found that between one-fifth to one-third of young Muslims show some signs of alienation from British society, meaning that they have a limited sense of patriotism and perceive there to be a conflict between loyalty to the Ummah[5] and to Britain. These young Muslims have also often been the victims of Islamophobia and they are especially angry about Iraq and Palestine. They are also distanced from traditional party politics. For Field (2011) there is a small minority of young Muslims, typically 5 to 10 per cent, who are very alienated. This means that they do not identify at all with Britain, and are ideologically committed to the overthrow of western society, even if only an extremely small number would actually use force themselves.

The discussions above highlight the ways in which the post 9/11 context is one rich in incompatibilities. Moreover, counter-terrorism post 9/11 is an arena of policy and practice that is seemingly comprised of binary opposites: covert versus overt counter-terrorism responses; community-focussed versus community-targeted approaches to counter-terrorism; the orientalist 'war on terror' and 'new terrorism' discourse creating 'insiders' and 'outsiders' in relation to sovereignty; Britishness versus Muslim identities and loyalties; and so forth. Added to this, there are additional stresses relating to organisational cultures. Whilst there is insufficient room here to address this issue fully, it is important to highlight that both statutory and non-statutory agencies are rife with dissenting viewpoints and with power struggles over strategy and practice. For instance, in the context of the police service in Northern Ireland, O'Rawe (2005) argues that whilst training is a key way of delivering institutional transformation to policing, training alone is insufficient in insti-gating a human rights culture. This is because 'there are powerful socialisation dynamics and unspoken messages that operate beyond the formal level' (O'Rawe, 2005: 946). Therefore, the police service may hold onto its subcultural values rather than embracing any change that training is attempting to

---

[5] The concept of 'Ummah' might be thought of as comprising a global Islamic community that super-sedes national or ethnic identities.

induce. Moreover, practitioners can ignore, circumvent, or even sabotage any attempts at implementing change (Oliver and Bartgis, 1998). Within counter-terrorism, there are state and non-state actors whose strategic and practical goals are focussed more on maintaining a conflictual approach rather than one that is based on conflict transformation. A conflictual approach accepts the 'war on terror' paradigm, does not question the notion of 'new terrorism' and operates by using counter-terrorism powers to target Muslim communities predominantly. An approach that embraces counter-terrorism as conflict transformation perhaps accepts that there are differing viewpoints and accounts regarding the causes and responses to 9/11 and its aftermath, seeking to build bridges between individuals and organisations with vastly differing perspectives and experiences.

Counter-terrorism as conflict transformation raises the interesting question of how, within a complex, conflictual environment, often comprised of struggles between different state and non-state actors, of struggles within and between communities, counter-terrorism work is carried out. In particular, since the July 2005 bombings in London in Britain, the Prevent strand within the British government counter-terrorism strategy has stressed the importance of the role of communities in helping to defeat terrorism. How, then, is community-based counter-terrorism work done, given the challenging socio-political environment? Are there lessons that we can take from those youth workers, police officers, probation officers and other practitioners, community members and young people themselves who have worked within a post 9/11 counter-terrorism context? Can we learn more about the everyday negotiations that take place, which are perhaps more aligned with conflict transformation than counter-terrorism as such?

Positionality and counter-terrorism practice as conflict transformation

One important thread running through the research data that I and my team have been collecting is that of the importance of a focus on identity for counter-terrorism practice. As a result of mass migration, globalisation and shifting national and international borders, alongside the significant presence of international ethnic and faith diasporas whose loyalties are not necessarily given to the nation-state in which individuals reside there has been some focus on identity. For example, Moisi (2009) has argued that within an increasingly globalised world, where nation-state borders are increasingly questioned and changing, struggles over identity have replaced ideological struggles. Identity has also been flagged up in relation to vulnerability to violent radicalisation, in that a lack of identity and a lack of belonging is viewed as increasing a person's vulnerability.

The notion of identity suggests sameness and difference – '... the notion of identity simultaneously establishes two possible relations of comparison between persons or things: *similarity*, on the one hand, and *difference*, on the other' (Jenkins, 2004: 3–4). An appreciation of sameness and difference is key for counter-terrorism practice, for those involved are often negotiating complex allegiances and loyalties, which themselves are likely to be shifting and unstable. At the same time, the actors involved may or may not understand their differences in relation to each other. Importantly, as identity is comprised of multiple positionalities in relation to 'race'/ethnicity, gender, religion, sexual orientation, disability, class and other subject positions, there are multiple ways in which connection and disconnection between people can be experienced. There are therefore myriad ways in which differences between people, groups and communities can be made manifest, presenting complex challenges for trust-building and partnership work in counter-terrorism. Alongside 'difference', multiple positionalities also enable 'sameness', in that they can be drawn on by those engaged in counter-terrorism in order to connect people, groups, institutions and communities. Within a counter-terrorism context this enables us to think about the ways in which connections can be made between state and non-state actors. For too long, state and non-state actors have been viewed as opposites, as being different and incompatible, when meaningful connections can be made between state and non-state actors. Implicit within many of the interviews that I and my research team have undertaken is the way in which individuals – whether as community members, police officers, youth workers or other practitioners – are aware of, and sometimes draw upon, their own positionalities when involved in work relating to counter-terrorism. As an example of this, below is an extract from and interview with a Muslim overt counter-terrorism police officer who uses his Muslim identity and his knowledge of Pakistan in order to raise questions about how vulnerability in relation to violent radicalisation is understood:

> Respondent: There was a closely discussed case by the security service, by the police, where an individual had gone to Pakistan and come back and there were, there were concerns about him because of his father's contacts and association with terrorism previously. And there were concerns of him going to Pakistan and having photographs taken with guns. He also changed his name.
>
> Interviewer: While in Pakistan?
>
> Respondent: While in Pakistan. And so this was being discussed about, the concerns about him and guns and whether he was being trained in Pakistan. But I said, 'Hang on a minute. That's a normal thing when you go to Pakistan … it's quite common. And because when I guess guns are not available and like any child you're curious and it's quite a cool thing to do and you do do it in Pakistan. But my concern is his name change. He's a Muslim kid who obviously had a Muslim name. Why does he need to change his name? I would look into the reason for that. And if his views are extreme, then we'll pick up any contributing behaviours or factors through that rather than his photographs with a gun.

In the above quotation, it is clear that the Muslim police officer is drawing on his Pakistani Muslim identity in order to articulate how it might be possible to identify risks associated with violent radicalisation. For this police officer, it is a change of name that is more significant than any photographs being taken in Pakistan with the boy holding a gun.

Whilst positionality might be thought of in relation to faith, ethnicity, gender and so on, positionality is also about credibility, and developing and maintaining this whilst engaging and partnering with wide-ranging actors and institutions. Credibility is a further important dimension to creating connections between people who are different sides of, or have different perspectives on, a conflict. Credible individuals on opposing or different sides are perhaps able to connect and work together for peace because it is their credibility that acts as the modus operandi through which trust and respect can be established.

The importance of credibility for counter-terrorism practice

Post 9/11 some of the counter terrorism initiatives that have been implemented might be more accurately thought of as peace-building initiatives.
Such initiatives draw on the credibility of the individuals concerned, where
credibility might be thought of as being independent, balanced and fair
within a world that is rife with power struggles. Being credible is about one's
identities in relation to faith, ethnicity, the 'street', politics and so forth. For
example, one community member who was interviewed has been involved
in peace-building work since before 9/11. The following is a quotation taken
from an interview with him which serves to illustrate the kind of work he has
been engaged in:

> … one of the things that I've been doing throughout my life is to fight
> extremism within Islam and Muslim communities. That's been something that
> I've been doing way, way before George Bush announced the war on terror. I
> mean I've been doing this since I was you know a high school graduate. I've
> been going round and giving lectures and talks and seminars and the such
> about how we should engage and I was pelted with stones by the likes of Abu
> Hamza … Because I was being accused of being sell out. Being someone who,
> you know, was an impostor to them and desecrated my religion and my faith
> which I think is absolute bull because of … how I understood Islam to be …
> up until 2001 we were winning many of the youngsters who I know harbour
> intentions of going abroad to some country fighting, you know, for Islam. They
> changed their minds because of what I used to tell them, because of the way in
> which I explained the Koran to them, the way in which I explained what they
> had to do here, how they should engage in politics, and they should engage in
> media. If they wanted to change things, this is how they do it. They don't go
> and, you know, kill themselves or whatever, that's not the way to change things.
> This is how you change things. You change people's minds and then things start
> changing. We were winning that battle.

This same community member further argues that the 'war on terror' has
made his work much more difficult as a result of the focus upon Muslim
identities and loyalties:

> But as soon as the war on terror was declared and the way it was declared, all
> of a sudden those same youngsters came back to us and said 'hang on, hang on,
> hang on, you've been telling us that we fit in here. Do we?' And what happened

in Leeds was that many, many youngsters who were good people, really good people, became absolutely disgusted and so angry and so frustrated that it was virtually useless for me to approach them again. I just couldn't go back to them. Because what do I say? What do I tell them? Come and engage with us? We are outcasts. It doesn't matter if I live all my life here, it doesn't matter that my best friends are Brits, white working class or this or that. It doesn't matter ultimately speaking, you're a Muslim … and you will be dealt in a way that, that makes me feel as though I am on the periphery of … society, I do not matter. And then you do what you do to Sadiq Khan, the MP, you bug him, and it just proves the fact that whatever you become, whoever you become, however far you reach in engaging with society, in working in politics, you will be seen as a Muslim and you will be seen as a possible subversive … And the likes of Abu Hamza, they win, without them even saying a word they win. You know, Abu Hamza is recruiting whilst he hasn't said a word over the past five years because he's been incarcerated in prison. But he's recruiting. We are recruiting on his behalf. The government is recruiting on his behalf. And that's where it becomes absolutely ludicrous, totally ridiculous.

This suggests that state responses to Muslims have challenged the credibility of those people involved in trying to reduce the potential for young Muslims to engage in violence: the message that Britain is an open and liberal society doesn't necessarily ring true when considering post 9/11 state-led security approaches. This is also an issue when thinking about state violence through warfare and other means and the mixed messages that young people receive in relation to the justified use of violence (McDonald, 2012).

The quotation below is drawn from an interview with a Muslim community member who runs a community centre for young people in a deprived part of London. He speaks about how his organisation challenges injustices, which may involve challenging the police, local authorities, community elders and young people themselves:

we're pretty much very challenging … We challenge police, we challenge local authorities, we challenge community elders, and we challenge those who portray a very distorted version of Islam, or false so you know … on the whole we are quite, we're quite an edgy group.

This same community member also talks about how this ability to challenge organisations and people gives him and his centre credibility:

... it gives us our credibility within that street environment and it allows our young people to feel comfortable to come and talk to us and discuss a range of issues. We're not promoting as such as a representative, we're promoting like if there's any inequalities or any injustice that's been carried out whether it's by the police or by the young people or by anybody we would be that access point and we would challenge that up or down. Depending on who's, who's been an issue and sometimes it's the police authorities have an issue with young people. So they'll come to us and we'll challenge down to the young people or the young people come to us, talk about the way they're being treated or the way they're being spoken to by authorities or by police or by their mosque imams, you know, and we challenge that, vice versa.

Furthermore, gaining credibility is about representing young powerless Muslims, the same groups of Muslims who are at risk from extremist groups:

So it's having that credibility that we are not representing ourselves but repre-senting them basically or somebody that can stand up against a system or power basically ... It's like an alternative to some of the more extremist groups who ... are sort of portraying themselves to be the leaders of the Muslim Ummah of today and challenging the system. We do that in a different way, for a more positive outcome. (H)

Credibility is not just an issue for community members working within a counter-terrorism context. This is also an issue for police officers and other practitioners. Counter-terrorism policing traditionally has adopted covert tactics, which means that being a counter-terrorism police officer carries with it a certain stigma, not least in the light of recent revelations in the media about a number of married undercover counter-terrorism police officers who had had sexual relationships with members of organisations that they had infiltrated (Ellen in *The Observer*, 2012). More recently, overt models of counter-terrorism policing have been introduced in which counter-terrorism police officers openly tell people who they are. Overt counter-terrorism police officers aim to build trust with community members. Police officers that I and my research team have interviewed are often aware of the stigma of a counter-terrorism identity, particularly since counter-terrorism policing has increasingly introduced overt counter-terrorism police officers who are openly telling people they are counter-terrorism officers. There can be dilemmas about telling people due to the stigma attached, as one police officer demonstrates:

I came in and you know, on day one this was my new job, and I'm now a Counter Terrorism Officer, and I've never been one, it's just where that role is created. And there were people within the council saying 'don't tell anyone that you're from the Counter Terrorism Unit, that will really cause some upset, just say you're a police officer, because you're not telling lies, you're a X Police Officer', and I said 'well no, because at some point it's going to come out, and if in six month's time people realise that I am in name a Counter Terrorism Officer they'll be "well why didn't you tell us that six months ago? You must be hiding something, you must be here with a different agenda". So from day one I've been the Counter Terrorism Officer who is seconded to the council to support and help you.

Below is a quotation from an overt counter-terrorism police officer who sees sharing personal information about aspects of his life as a way of engaging and building trust with community members:

It's not easy, it's not easy to go to people and say, you know, 'I work for the counter-terrorism unit' which is what we're supposed … we have to do … And you need to be able to talk about, you know, yesterday, your kids, the fact that you're having a baby. You know, all that kind of … not just go in and go "well actually, I'm preventing violent extremism and I …", you know, because that's not what it's about.

In the quotation below, another overt counter-terrorism police officer talks about how he negotiates wearing his police uniform with communities:

I normally do ask them, 'Would you mind if I came in uniform or would you prefer me in plain clothes?' and they're normally very open and ask you either way. If they want you in plain clothes they normally say why and the majority of the time they don't, they don't mind you being in uniform err depending on what capacity or what reason you're actually visiting them … mostly they, they're actually very pleased that you come in plain clothes and you accommodate their wish, which is quite nice for them because we're not forcing ourselves on to them.

This same officer speaks about her Muslim identity and how this has influenced her decision to become an overt counter-terrorism police officer, and how being both a Muslim and a police officer within the counter-terrorism field can be challenging, suggesting the intersectionality between a police identity and a Muslim identity:

I put in for it (counter-terrorism) because (a) I believed I had the skills for what the job description required and secondly, I was interested in terrorism and, and the myth surrounding the Muslim community. And because I'm a Muslim officer I believe that not just as an officer, I've also got a duty as Muslim to, to actually help the community understand what it is and being a police officer you're stuck between the two lines really, because you've got procedure and your job and your duties but you've also got your beliefs you know it's not true. So you want to make a difference but in a positive way. But also make the organisation understand the community better. Hence why I applied for it.

Being a Muslim can open access to parts of the community that are inaccessible for non-Muslims, as the following Muslim lawyer suggests:

I'm conscious of the fact that doors open for me that wouldn't necessarily open for a non-Muslim prosecutor or non-Muslim officers. And if I have any influence I should use it.

Muslim counter-terrorism officers take risks in that they can become the targets of rumour and gossip from within their own communities. Below is a quotation from a Muslim overt counter-terrorism police officer who speaks about the kind of trust he had built with local Muslims:

… and the reaction from the community as well that because I'd got a certain amount of credibility within the community and including people that I haven't met and things before, it goes back to how you come across. People can very easily judge whether you are being genuine or sincere in what you say and do. And I was certainly very open about the work, what I was doing … And people believed us. … and people trusted us and we still maintain that trust.

This same police officer then continues to explain how one member of his local Muslim community was speaking out against him because he was a counter-terrorism police officer:

The only setback I had was that one particular very influential guy had spoken about me in very negative, I have to say, had lied about me in terms of certain conversations and things and I could prove it. So much so to the extent that he was calling me a fool and a hypocrite in certain circles that he was holding … and it shows the extent of this guy because my sister was at that talk and she was pregnant at the time. Now he had made life very difficult for myself in particular, for my wife and children and including my mother. And I had to go through a few months of very hard times where I was being blamed by my younger brothers and sisters who'd been married and were settling in with kids and things and they're well known in the community. And so that ... but thankfully I happen to know that's in the past and this particular person is, you know, good relationships with me at the moment. But I don't bring the issue up. But I can forgive but I can't never forget that.

Clearly, this illustrates how an overt counter-terrorism police officer and members of his family can be stigmatised by rumours that are spread by disaffected individuals from within communities.

Credibility is also about understanding, and even coming from and/or being part of, street-level urban dynamics. A significant number of the people that I and my research team have interviewed spoke about the relevance of 'the street' for the work that they do. For one youth worker, adopting or drawing upon a 'street' positionality is about your credibility in relation to the young people that you are working with, most of whom live within urban poor environments:

> Well the street is your, is your credibility, is your kudos, is your ability to gain that respect in the eyes of young people initially. And I'd say the majority of our kids it probably is a prerequisite. You have to have that element of respect and kudos for them to be able to, to, to come and, you know, give you time of day ...

This same youth worker also talks about how street credibility is often about showing off items associated with material success, like nice cars:

> So you could turn up in a Porsche and instantly you've got cred ... because you're in a Porsche and that's it; that's what they want to aspire to. These are their ideas of success. You've obviously made it. You're a gangster because you've got a Porsche. So in the world where all our kids want to be gangsters, and I think they are already living in a ghetto, that's your street, that's your cred, that's your kudos ... it's not a wonderful thing but it is real.

However, young people can go beyond this rather superficial kind of respect, based upon materialism, to develop a more meaningful relationship with youth workers:

> What can change after a certain amount of time is that then it moves on from that and it becomes slightly more, you know, less superficial and it moves on to more of a trusting relationship and then you don't need to rely so much on the fast car, the slick clothes and you can dress like me you know. KA1

For another youth worker, 'street knowledge' is about understanding the dynamics of communities within poor urbanised areas and their links to violent radicalisation:

> Street cred and some of the baddest people we've had from this area are the ones who end up in Belmarsh and come out with very Islamic, very extremist ideological views. So what we also have to understand about this is leadership and community dynamics, how communities work. Gang culture.

For this same youth worker, to run an effective 'street-based' community intervention programme, it is important to identify and influence community and gang leaders. Having the right leadership is key:

> I set up this programme called the Diamond Programme and we believe, I believe that every community has diamonds, gems and pearls. Now in order to run effective programmes, you've got to influence your diamonds because your diamonds are like your leaders, yeah, and leaders make or break decisions. So it doesn't matter how much money the Home Office provide on this that, on that, if you haven't got the right leadership in communities, if you've not got the buy-in from the community, you'll never get close to this issue, you'll never get close to addressing this issue because you've got to have local intelligence, you've got to have local knowledge.

This youth worker also talks about the importance of coming from the same environment as the people with whom you are engaging and working:

> People who have killed people come in and hand themselves into XXX (community project), people involved in all kinds of atrocities will come and hand themselves in to us before the authorities. Why? Because we've got that respect of the community. Why have we got that respect of the community? Not because we're any better than anyone else, because we come from the community, we're part of the community, the community trusts us ... Because the community, you're part of that community, you've not jumped down on parachutes and said we're setting this up and setting that up, it doesn't work, it doesn't work.

For this same youth worker, a 'street' positionality is about being angry with the state, and how violence can be associated with glamour:

> ... there's a confidence against the system and if you're in a situation where the system has let you down, believe me, it's not hard to alter that mindset at all 'cos

people are desperate, you know, people are desperate ... you have to understand it because there's something very attractive to the street guy of Handsworth, of Brixton, of Moss Side to Islam because all the kind of concept that Islamic terrorism kind of holds ... the whole glamorisation, you know, weaponry, it's all attractive.

It is important to stress that for those wanting to access and work with young people from within deprived urban 'street' areas, it is important to have 'street' credibility and to have facilities that young people are attracted to, as one community member argues:

> I think it's mainly by having a bit of background within the street environment myself. But also being well recognised and well respected in the community. But I also think our key engaging point will have been the hook, which was the gym ... which it's a Muslim you know designed gym.

Therefore, police officers wishing to implement programmes of intervention with key groups have to draw upon the skills and expertise of credible community members, who may not necessarily be traditional community leaders. This presents a risk for those community members who implement programmes linked to policing initiatives, for their links with police may harm their credibility, as the following quotation from a Muslim community member demonstrates:

> With this programme, some of these young people may volunteer to be involved in some preventative work, so they may facilitate some of the activities that XXX (overt counter-terrorism police officers) do for example, because that's been something that XX have brought ... brought to me.

> Interviewer: Like football stuff?

> Football stuff or delivering the DVD Act. Now for example 'cos obviously they see that when a police officer's delivering some of these workshops, obviously it's gonna be tainted ... so they want somebody from the community to deliver it. So young people may have a role and I think, again, it's just one of those things that they may lose the respect and the trust in the community as soon as they start delivering programmes that are normally delivered by counter-terrorism officers or by uniformed officers.

The notion of the co-production of security has gained increasing research interest, with the idea that policing is a shared responsibility between police, communities and other stakeholders. It is important to highlight that the interviews I and my team have undertaken would seem to suggest that within the highly sensitive and conflict-ridden counter-terrorism arena there are times when programmes and initiatives have to be led by community members. This means that security is not necessarily co-produced, or shared, but rather is driven by community members, who necessarily have to take the lead as a result of their credibility. The following community member talks about the ongoing contact he and his organisation have with young people, thereby enabling a deep understanding and appreciation of the issues surrounding young people's lives:

> ... but also the centre that we have here it allows young people to come in at any time of the day, you know, or evening, to engage and play pool or you know get involved in some activities but also to come and discuss some of the issues that they're experiencing, or their friends are experiencing or also to sort of inform us of what's going on basically ... but we're also working within a street environment, we have a lot of connections within local schools as well, with young people. So you know we find it very easy to access young people on the street, in schools and the communities behind the walls of silence ... t's our, our specialist sort of field.

Another community member talks about the expertise he has built around vulnerability to violent radicalisation purely as a result of his lived experiences:

> ... I've been in the Brixton community, I converted there in 1990 and at that time quite a few of my colleagues converted as well. And what we realised as young Muslims then is that Brixton mosque attracted a lot of attention from various elements in the Muslim community. Why? We realised because it was the only or first convert-led mosque and still remains a convert-led mosque. So we saw all sorts of elements coming in to the mosque and before I became chairman we would have Nation of Islam showing a presence there. The Qadiyyanis would come there, you would have the Taqfiri jihadi, extreme jihadi methodology there. And we started learning the Salafi methodology from some of the teachers there who were not an authority but they were well respected members of the community. We then started trying to elucidate what was the correct methodology and so you can't have all of these practices in one mosque ...

This same community member also talks about how, when he became Chairman of the local mosque, he decided that the mosque had to have a consistent and precise ideology, one that takes a stance against Jihadist extremists:

> When I came to a position of chairman I said 'I think the only way that the mosque could function was to have a single ideology, we would welcome others in, it didn't matter who they were but they would see that this mosque is following one single ideology.' And that's one of the things that I started implementing in 1994. And in doing that we've had to make stances against some of the other groups so what we did, the most prolific of them were the Taqfiris, this Jihadist extreme understanding because jihad is a noble word but they had an extreme understanding of jihad and they started coming and praying amongst the community saying we'll teach you Arabic and as they won their trust started talking about the regimes and the, basically the infidel regimes in the Middle East and all sorts of concepts that I heard before I became chairman.

He also speaks about how he was able to use the pulpit to counter extremist rhetoric within the community:

> I was now able to address on the pulpit, in the Khutbas, in our written work, in our study circles so we were starting to realise in where this was going, looking at some of the fatwas that they were giving outside. In Algeria for example we saw fatwas that the police and all their families were infidels, they could be killed, and we were hearing this in the mosque. And I was saying 'no, this is a false understanding of Islam' so they realised we'd been fighting this fight.

He then stresses that his mosque was open twenty-four hours a day, thereby allowing for a solid community response to vulnerability:

> We saw all of this happening and they were expounding these views amongst friends of ours and we saw our friends going in that direction. So not only would it be robust rebuttal and ideological – erm – refutation, we have friends that we had to spend time with, we were having people sleep over in the mosque during those times because they needed a place of refuge. So we had to make sure that the extreme ideology wasn't being propagated amongst these individuals as well so a lot of patience, care, time and you might think Brixton mosque was one of the mosques that stayed open 24 hours a day, seven days a week. We didn't close.

Time and time again, interviews point to community members showing remarkable leadership skills within counter-terrorism. This is about community members deciding what actions need to be taken, despite putting themselves at considerable risk, particularly in relation to their credibility. It is about knowing what needs to be done and making decisions. The following is an extract from an interview with a Muslim community member who was on the ground with Muslim youth during an EDL march, persuading them not to engage in violent actions against the EDL:

> I actually again on the day I managed to speak to young people and dissuaded about a group of 20 to leave you know, the area and go back, because I knew them, just happened to know them, so they left. So again, that relationship building, the police were seeing that happening ... the silver commander on the ground was about to do something and I was there at the time and I felt that if he'd done that it wouldn't have worked, so he pulled me to the side and we spoke.

As indicated above, not only did this community member dissuade Muslim youth from engaging in potentially provocative and even violent activities, but also he was keen to persuade a senior police officer into taking a different course of action. This demonstrates leadership: building peace requires leadership skills. This means drawing upon, as well as taking risks with, one's own credibility. The question this raises is what motivates people to draw upon, and risk, their credibility to undertake such work? Preventing violence is a key motivation, and preventing young people from being incarcerated and punished is another. Another significant motivating factor appears to faith, and in a post-9/11 context where counter-terrorism involves Muslim communities, this means Islam as a rich source of motivation, inspiring individuals to work within challenging contexts. For instance, one Muslim lawyer explains that:

> And yes, does my faith come into it? Yeah, my faith is I believe in Islam and justice and I believe it's important that there is justice for victims and witnesses and for people who are suspected of crimes who aren't guilty. And so I, I, one of the reasons why I'm doing my job is about being able to, erm, do that, make a difference in people's lives.

A Muslim community member argues the following:

> I mean it's your ethics, it's your moral compass, it's, you know, I want to be professional, I want to do a job properly and it's all because you know as a Muslim I feel I owe a duty to the, to my ... if you feel like you're accountable to something higher ... if you need that justice you have to be just too in all your

relations so you have to be just towards your family, their own certain duties, if your employers are paying you a wage you have to be, you know, you have to do your job properly, I'm accountable to my cases.

The research data reveals that, contrary to the common assumption that commitment to Islamic values and religious doctrines is the root cause of terrorism, religion in these cases provides a stronger commitment and a feeling of moral responsibility – *a duty* or *a religious obligation* – as put by many, to help solve the problem of violence committed in the name of Islam, and to build bridges and form positive relations with other British communities.

Conclusion

This chapter raises many important issues. It leads us to think about counter-terrorism in new and more challenging ways. Where there are multiple claims over 'truth', multiple experiences of, and perspectives upon, a post-9/11 world, it is important to consider counter-terrorism as conflict transformation, as this is a more accurate understanding of real-world dynamics. This chapter illustrates that within the post-9/11 environment there are numerous and ongoing struggles and contestations. At the core of counter-terrorism as conflict transformation is the notion of credibility, for this determines the extent to which a person's message, viewpoint or initiative really can influence behaviour, particularly amongst those deemed at risk of vulnerability to violent radicalisation. Credibility is about a person's positionality, about how a person draws upon their multiple identities in order to build trust and relationships with their key audiences and potential partners. Credibility can be challenging, for this is about being prepared to challenge dominant power structures in order to try to secure social justice, in a world characterised by social injustice. Credibility can be frightening for power elites, for often those in power have gained their privileges through the perpetuation, or at least ignorance, of social injustice. Credibility can play an important transformative role within conflict precisely because this is about maintaining integrity and trust despite considerable pressures to conform to dominant norms that may include repression, human rights abuses, violence or its promotion. Credibility can be an important resource through which to build and maintain important connections with wide-ranging actors for the purposes of conflict transformation, of offering peaceful responses to social norms and practices that are unjust and even violent. State responses to terrorism can impact negatively on the credibility that state and non-state actors have worked hard to build, and a key lesson that appears to come from the data presented in this chapter is that it is important to maintain credibility through showing strong leadership skills, through robustly challenging injustice, even if that involves questioning dominant state-led counter-terrorism responses that may be supported by powerful governing elites. The next chapter takes this analysis further by focusing on the role of community policing in relation to counter-terrorism as conflict transformation.

Bibliography

BBC2 (2006) *9/11 The Conspiracy Files*, 7 December 2006, http://news.bbc.co.uk/1/hi/programmes/6160775.stm (accessed 15 August 2012).

BBC News Magazine (2011) '9/11 Conspiracy Theories', 29 August 2011, http://www.bbc.co.uk/news/magazine-14665953 (accessed 15 August 2012).

Choudhury, T. and Fenwick, H. (2011) *The Impact of Counter-Terrorism Measures on Muslim Communities*, London: Equality and Human Rights Commission.

Ellen, B. (2012) 'Police Spies Must Keep Everything Firmly Zipped' *The Observer* 17 June 2012, www.guardian.co.uk/commentisfree/2012/jun/17/barbara-ellen-undercover-police-sex (accessed 15 August 2012).

Field, C. (2011) 'Young British Muslims since 9/11: a Composite Attitudinal Profile' *Religion, State and Society*, Vol. 39 (2/3) pp. 159–76.

Hewitt, S., Spalek, B. and McDonald, L. Z. (2012) 'Dissent, Protest and Conflict within and between Communities,' *Summary Report*, AHRC Connected Communities Programme.

Hickman, M., Silvestri, S. and Nickels, N. (2011) 'Suspect Communities' ? Counter-Terrorism Policy, the Press and the Impact on Irish and Muslim Communities in Britain London: Metropolitan University, www.city.ac.uk/__data/assets/pdf_file/0005/96287/suspect-communities-report-july2011.pdf (accessed 2 April 2013).

Home Office (2011) Prevent Strategy London: HMSO, http://www.gov.uk/government/uploads/system/uploads/attachment_data/file/97976/prevent-strategy-review.pdf (accessed 2 April 2013).

Jenkins, R. (2004) *Social Identity,* London: Routledge.

Jutila, M. (2006) 'Desecuritizing minority rights: against determinism', *Security Dialogue*, 37, 2, pp. 167–85.

Kundnani, A. (2009) *Spooked! How not to prevent violent extremism*, London: Institute of Race Relations.

McDonald, L. Z. (2012) 'Engaging Young People within a Counter-Terrorism Context' in: B.Spalek (ed.) *Counter-Terrorism: community-based approaches to terror crime* Basingstoke: Palgrave MacMillan, pp. 90–136.

McGovern, M. (2010) *Countering Terror or Counter-Productive? Comparing Irish and British Muslim Experiences of Counter-Insurgency Law and Policy.* Report of a Symposium held in Cultúrlann McAdam Ó Fiaich, Falls Road, Belfast, 23–24 June 2009, Lancashire: Edge Hill University.

Moisi, D. (2009) *The Geo Politics of Emotion*, London: the Bodley Head.

Mythen, G. and Walklate, S. (2006) 'Criminology and Terrorism', *British Journal of Criminology* 46 (3): pp. 379–98.

Oliver, M. W. and Bartgis, E. (1998) 'Community policing: a conceptual framework', *Policing: An International Journal of Police Strategies & Management,* Vol. 21 (3) pp. 490–509.

O'Rawe, M. (2005) 'Human Rights and Police Training in Transitional Societies: exporting the lessons of Northern Ireland' *Human Rights Quarterly*, Vol. 27, pp. 943–68.

Pantazis, C. and Pemberton, S. (2009) 'From the "Old" to the "New Suspect" Community: Examining the Impacts of Recent UK Counter-Terrorist Legislation', *British Journal of Criminology* 49 (5): 646–66.

Poynting, S. and Mason, V. (2008) 'The New Integrationism, the State and Islamophobia: Retreat from Multiculturalism in Australia', *International Journal of Law, Crime and Justice* 36 (4): 230–46.

Silk, D., O'Rawe, M. and Spalek, B. (eds) (2013) *Preventing Ideological Violence: communities, police and case studies of "success"* Basingstoke: Palgrave MacMillan.

Spalek, B., El-Awa, S. and McDonald, L. Z. (2009) 'Engagement and Partnership Work in a Counter-Terrorism Context', University of Birmingham.

Spalek, B. and McDonald, L. Z. (2010) 'Anti-Social Behaviour Powers and the Policing of Security' *Social Policy and Society*, Vol. 9 (1), pp. 123–33.

—(2011) 'Preventing Religio-Political Violent Extremism Amongst Muslim Youth: a study exploring police-community partnership', University of Birmingham.

3

Community Policing within a Counter-Terrorism Context: Understanding Police and Community Engagement

Introduction

In relation to ordinary, everyday, crime, community policing has raised many questions about whether it is a philosophy, a model of practice, an organisational strategy, a de-centralised approach to problem-solving or a combination of these, there being no clear agreement on its meaning (Chavez, 2012). Community policing in relation to counter-terrorism has also generated substantial research and policy interest, with emotive and politicised reverberations often underpinning the debates. Normative assumptions around how to create a more secure society influence the ways in which community policing, and community-based approaches more generally, have been conceptualised, critiqued and researched in relation to countering terrorism.

In Britain, a pioneer of community policing for counter-terrorism has been Dr Robert Lambert who, after 9/11, created the Muslim Contact Unit (MCU). This is a small counter-terrorism unit with the London Metropolitan Police Service which drew upon community policing principles in its more overt approach to counter-terrorism. Dr Lambert was a former undercover police officer who had directly experienced the damage that infiltration and spying can sometimes do, both on communities and on the police officers who undertake this work. Dr Lambert has therefore been keen to create a new way of dealing with terrorism, one that is more open and accountable to communities. The work of the MCU has been controversial, but not because of the community policing model at the heart of its approach. Rather, the MCU has been controversial for approaching Salafi and Islamist communities as partners and not suspects even though, within government and some policy circles, these groups are often perceived as potentially dangerous radicals (Lambert, 2011).

Another key figure in this area is Professor Martin Innes, who has been a significant advocate for the role of Neighbourhood Policing (a model of community policing) in relation to counter-terrorism, which underpins the Prevent agenda in Britain. Professor Innes' work has often been sponsored by the Association of Chief Police Officers (ACPO), which has been a strong supporter and instigator of the Prevent agenda. Other key authors in this debate include Professor Deborah Ramirez, Wayne Hanniman, Dr Dan Silk, Dr Basia Spalek, Dr Laura Zahra McDonald and Dr Salwa El-Awa. For these individuals, community policing has predominantly been viewed as a way of building bridges between securitised and ostracised Muslim communities and non-Muslim communities in Britain, the US and in Canada, as well as offering the potential to develop new and radical ways of approaching counter-terrorism, an arena that has traditionally been characterised by secrecy and by human rights abuses. Another key author to highlight here is Arun Kundnani who, in 2009, wrote *Spooked, How Not to Prevent Violent Extremism*. This report accused the Prevent agenda in Britain of being a government-legitimated spying on Muslim communities, and of alienating Muslim communities rather than convincing them of the need for their engagement in responding to terrorism.

This chapter explores the work referred to above more closely, in order to highlight some of the key claims made by the authors, and to examine the main points of contestation. It also draws upon empirical data, collected by the author and her team between 2007 and 2012, in relation to Muslim community and police officer experiences of police–community relations. In analyses of policing generally, and in the literature that has focussed on examining police–community relations, the complexity of the dynamics between police and communities is often missing. In the sociological and criminological literature on policing, it is often assumed that there is tension between police and communities, particularly for those communities who have historically had difficult relationships with police. Nonetheless, within any conflict, important alliances can be built between individuals who may occupy different sides or positions in relation to the ongoing struggle. In the peace-building and conflict-resolution research material, which is based predominantly on post-conflict societies and/or societies in transition, there is little in-depth understanding of police and community relations; policing is examined and attention often tends to be drawn to organisational changes taking place within police services rather than any actual experiences of the interactions between police officers and community members. Trying to understand something as complex, fluid and dynamic as police and community engagement is deeply problematic, for the data that I and my research team have been gathering indicates vastly differing experiences and perceptions of police and community engagement. Trying to link these different narratives together to present a coherent framework of analysis is perhaps impossible. This is an important point, given that due to the politicised arena of counter-terrorism policing, dominant elites often decide on a particular set of policies and practices and then fit research and empirical data around these in order to validate their particular approaches and rationales. The data presented in this chapter has not been tampered with in order to promote a particular philosophy, ideology or political standpoint. The fragments of data presented are real-world, human experiences, and as such are invaluable to our understanding of community policing in relation to counter-terrorism.

Community policing and counter-terrorism: Some key debates

The work of Professor Martin Innes (2006; 2007; 2011) has been especially influential upon policing within a counter-terrorism context. For Innes, counter-terrorism policing is about harnessing the potential of Neighbourhood Police officer teams who have ongoing engagement with local communities, and who respond to the crime-fighting needs of local communities (Innes et al., 2007). Neighbourhood policing is one of the most significant models of policing to be implemented in Britain in recent years. It is about areas having local police teams that can most effectively respond to community needs as a result of their presence and relationships with community members. Innes

(2006) has argued that under the neighbourhood policing model, which contains elements of community-based policing, in responding to individuals' routine security concerns around issues such as anti-social behaviour or crime police officers will be more likely to persuade community members of the benefits of assisting them. Neighbourhood policing has been explicitly linked to counter-terrorism activities in that it is argued that 'neighbourhood policing is a process that can be harnessed to establish the presence of any suspicions about potential terrorist activities' (Innes, 2006: 14). Moreover, it is argued that the indicators for suspecting terror activities may be subtle and not all known to any one person. Therefore, neighbourhood policing should be well placed to handle the diffuse information coming from different individuals, due to the beneficial 'weak community ties' developed between police and community members through such a policing model (Innes, 2006: 14). Localism appears to be a key theme that underpins much of Innes' work in relation to counter-terrorism policing. In line with this, Innes and his research colleagues use a situational model of violent radicalisation. They argue that 'a degree of situational configuration to respond to local circumstances is both necessary and desirable' (Innes et al., 2011: 9) and that, moreover, inhibiting the onset of radicalisation requires targeted local interventions for the factors in radicalisation itself are often local issues (Innes et al., 2011). This localised approach resonates with the review of the Prevent Strategy 2011, in which it is acknowledged that the Government is committed to a fundamental shift of power away from central government to communities, families and individuals, through Big Society. However, Innes' almost exclusive focus upon local dynamics and local grievances may be problematic in that it does not sufficiently take into consideration global factors, and thus represents a de-politicisation of the issues at stake. Local grievances, local factors, may have their roots in international dynamics, in geo-political power plays involving nation-states. Innes' approach potentially places police officers within an overly narrow lens, an overly naive position that can perhaps put police–community relations under greater strain.

Another key theme within the work of Innes is that of police officers working with communities to respond not only to their concerns about crime, but also to adopt a 'hearts and minds' approach that attempts to influence people's attitudes and beliefs so that they are less likely to support (tacitly or explicitly) 'either the means or ends of those groups espousing the use of violence' (Innes et al., 2007:13). This theme draws upon the field of terrorism studies, in that some discussion features here of the role of community in endorsing or supporting terrorism. Crenshaw (1981) has, for example, argued that whilst there may be a lack of popular support at the start of any conflict, terrorists can mobilise widespread support, and public allegiance, during the course of the conflict. For Anderson (2011), it is important to consider violence in relation to how it is committed for or in the name of communities – at local, national and transnational levels – as popular support is necessary for social change. The position taken by the West Midlands Police Authority in relation to Al Qaeda (AQ) linked or influenced terrorism and Muslim communities also reflects this:

Beyond the small core of active or potentially active extremists, and the members of the radical political movements that surround them, there appears to be a much larger group of British Muslims who are morally ambivalent and who are unwilling explicitly to condemn the violent extremists. Polls carried out by a number of respected survey organisations indicate that this figure may be between 10 and 20 per cent of the total Muslim population in Britain. (WMPA, 2008: 9)

Post 9/11, with the counter-terrorism focus being almost exclusively upon AQ-linked or influenced terrorism, the general literature in terrorism studies on passive or active support of communities for terrorism has perhaps too easily been applied almost exclusively to Muslim communities. This has created a situation whereby minority Muslim communities in the West, their identities, allegiances, support for the use of violence and so forth, have been almost exclusively the focus of policy and research interest, above all other communities. This narrow focus, the passive or active support of Muslim communities in relation to terrorism, and moreover, police interest in the 'hearts and minds' of Muslims, is problematic from a number of perspectives. The focus on active or passive support for terrorism amongst Muslims often fails to consider the wider social and political factors that underpin any such support. Schmid (2007) has argued that social factors like poverty or disenfranchisement can play a role in community support for terrorism. A study by Ray et al. (2004), examining the motivations behind offenders of race-hate crimes, found that the economic context was crucial because the offenders lived in segregated communities in areas of high unemployment. Industries that had previously employed their parents and grandparents had collapsed. This research would suggest that it is important to consider the wider social and economic factors behind violence and terrorism, especially when considering late modernity and the social and economic processes that have led to increasing separation and exclusion, creating a world of uncertainty and risk (Young, 1999). The 'hearts and minds' strategy, as advocated by Innes, therefore potentially focuses attention almost exclusively on support for violence within communities, without taking into consideration broader social and economic factors underpinning that support. At the same time, within the post 9/11 context the focus has been almost exclusively upon Muslim communities, which is problematic for a number of reasons. Much of the Muslim world is governed by non-legitimate elites, as the Arab Spring has clearly illustrated. The role of Western governments in helping to maintain these elites when pursuing their own 'national interests' of course will create grievances within Muslim communities in the West, who seek greater social justice for peoples of the Middle East and Asia. The danger with the exclusive focus on the 'hearts and minds' of Muslim communities is that these communities become pathologised and seen as problematic, without due consideration of wider global politics. As previously argued, a new dichotomy has been created, in which Muslims are subject to categorisation into 'moderates' and 'radicals', with theological and political beliefs or 'values', and their related grievances deemed either legitimate or not (Spalek and McDonald, 2010). Any groups deemed 'radical' are, if not constructed as potential violent actors, categorised as creating an environment in which terrorist activity may be inspired or flourish. Labels such as 'Salafi' and 'Islamist' – applied to a wide range of non-violent Muslim organisations and individuals – have been used to conflate a wide range of theological and political positions not only inaccurately with each other, but with AQ-type philosophy and violence. This has the potential to alienate and disenfranchise large sections of Muslim communities, who will share a sense of exclusion through reductionist interpretations of complex identities and allegiances (Spalek and McDonald, 2010). Interestingly, during the trial of Anders Breivik, responsible for the killing of 77 people on 22 July 2011 in Norway, there was some media discussion about the extent to which Breivik's ideology features in mainstream society – the attacks on multiculturalism, the fear of difference, racism and so forth (Moore, 2012). It is therefore unsurprising that Muslim communities have felt themselves to be unfairly scrutinised, when extreme views are present within all communities and across all society. Work by Spalek, El-Awa and McDonald (2009) illustrates how local initiatives aimed at countering terrorism can embrace Islamic religious beliefs and practices. Religion can be used directly in terror-prevention strategies to pull those deemed at risk away from vulnerability. At the same time religion can be a motivating factor for communities to partner the state in countering terrorism. Therefore, it is important that Islam itself and Muslim identities and theological positionalities are not problematised.

This discussion illustrates the complex terrain for counter-terrorism policing when pursuing a 'hearts and minds' approach and raises the question whether counter-terrorism policing should take this approach, since there is the danger that it targets ideology rather than violence. Another danger with the almost exclusive focus on Muslim communities is that political positions on Palestine, Afghanistan and so forth, and theological positions in relation to issues such as Sharia, can be the target of policing, in addition to the policing of violence. This raises the question of whether this should be the role of policing, especially when considering the roots of community policing under Robert Peel, who argued that the public are the police and the police are the public. Within the Prevent Review strategy 2011 there is an increased focus on extremism rather than violent extremism, and so there are real dangers involved here for the police in terms of the potential to go beyond the remit of policing into the more ill-defined and diffuse realms of 'extremism'. If thinking about the role of policing as one of persuasion in relation to ideology, is this not the traditional focus of the secret services rather than police agencies? Could this potentially damage police and community relations, particularly amongst those communities most targeted by 'hearts and minds' strategies?

There is also significant attention in the work of Innes to the issue of police–community engagement in relation to counter-terrorism. For Innes (2006), strategic engagement is about soft power, about police officers using engagement strategically for two key purposes: to counter rumours within communities, and also as an intelligence feed for the police. The theme of countering rumours has emerged from the data that my research team and I have collected, with police officers talking about the importance of being aware of any misinformation that may be circulating within communities and being able to robustly challenge this:

> There's a bit of urban myth around it as well, you know, some people get stopped and, you know, word will get round the community that, you know, their copy of the Koran was manhandled and a dog trampled all over their suitcase and, you know, none of which is necessarily true, but it's ... it shows the potential for those incidents to get ... to cause a lot of grievances and misreporting and misinformation within the communities.

Innes et al. (2007: 13) refer to an 'eyes and ears' strategy which is intended to persuade citizens to act as intelligence assets for the authorities. Interestingly, Innes does not raise the issue of the historical tensions between police and minority communities, treating citizens as though they are divorced from their individual and group identities in relation to 'race'/ethnicity, gender, faith, sexual orientation and so forth.

The representation of minority groups within the police service has been a serious issue, with the under-representation of minority ethnic and Muslim communities within the police in particular raising concerns (Rowe, 2004); yet for Innes et al. (2007) all citizens appear the same. Some of the police officers that we interviewed have indicated the real value of having Muslim or minority ethnic police officers involved in counter-terrorism work. For example, the following quotation from a counter-terrorism officer emphasises the importance of police services employing Muslims and Black and Minority Ethnic (BME) officers more generally, especially in a context where trust placed in the police by minority ethnic communities may be low:

> it's about cultural understanding and it's also about recognising where the police service is in relation to the minority communities ... if you can look at every major poll the number, the level of trust and confidence within the BME communities is lower than the trust and confidence in the white community. So it's about actually having Muslim officers who understand the community, the community are going to trust and have confidence in.

The same police officer also observes that Muslim and BME officers can effectively build relationships with those communities:

> The officers have a role in improving relationships with the community ... and it's just simple things, you know. If you end up with a, having a Muslim

officer, a BME officer who can stand up after a police operation to explain what's happened and it will send out a very, very positive message to the community. Whereas at the moment invariably you have er, with the lack of Muslims within counter terrorism command, very low, very low numbers, 1 or 2%, if you have a an operation then you will have no Muslims virtually within the operation and if you do they have a very, very peripheral role, and then in addition to that you then have the whole of the operation, the media, the follow up, the community reassurance, being done by white officers who …

The following quotation is from a counter-terrorism police officer who worked within the MCU, who argues that, as the remit of the police unit was to approach Muslim communities, it was important for the unit to employ Muslim police officers:

> … part of developing the Muslim Contact Unit approach, we are approaching Muslim communities, we were quite clearly, you know, we weren't approaching other communities and Muslim police officers that had great integrity in local communities were obviously a great asset.

When Innes writes about strategic engagement between police officers and community members, an issue that he leaves out is that of the difference between superficial and real engagement. From the interviews that we conducted, it seems that what community members value is 'real engagement', and they are much less enthusiastic about superficial engagement. The following is a quotation from a Muslim man who explains that there are good and bad examples of police and community engagement:

> Muslim relations with the police are very much in many cases, depending on which area, they vary from good, very good to bad, to extremely bad … and it depends on the level of expertise. So for instance with the Met and the MCU X has developed a really good example of how things can work. With Y it's an example of how things can not work where you superficially engage, below the surface nobody trusts anybody, and below the surface nobody is willing to cooperate, and below the surface the problems are getting worse and worse … it's just a rubber stamp for the police in many areas. So there's no hope left. And eventually these young youth get so disaffected they just go off onto themselves, and then we hear about extremist actions being taken and we say why, you know?

The following is a quotation from a Muslim woman speaking about communities looking for answers from the police but often not getting, in her opinion, satisfactory responses:

> After 7/7 for example is, you know, you would have community meetings, you'd have men and women come, they can ask questions to the Imam or even police representatives were there, so they can kind of ask the questions freely and I think often, from what I recall, some of the questions that were asked to the police were not answered, they did not receive satisfactory answers back from the police, because it felt like okay, we're asking you a question but you're not actually listening to what the real question is. You know, they regurgitate a certain answer that has been written up by lawyers and things like that.

This same Muslim woman speaks about communities seeking sincerity from the police:

> Whereas what the community is looking for is sincere empathy maybe for the situation that the Muslim community is in and proof, some sort of proof to show that you are not, not … if one feels like as if, or a lot of Muslims I think, feel like as if there's an attitude of stigmatising the Muslims and, you know, as a whole community and persecuted because, you know, obviously the increase in certain stop and search has increased, the amount of violence against Muslim women with their scarves, and their scarves have been pulled off and things like that, obviously increased so there was not enough done at police level and at the level of the authorities who had responsibility to make sure there was no backlash and things against the Muslims. There wasn't enough of that done to reassure, support and reassure the community that there was that support from the police.

This woman clearly stresses the violence that has been committed against Muslim women and her opinion that there has not been enough done to provide Muslims with the reassurance they need to be able to feel safe from hate crime.

The following quotation is from an interview with a male Muslim community member, who suggests that 'easy engagement', whereby community members agree with police approaches and do not really question these, is what police often look for:

> The police actually didn't also want to really have difficult times in these meetings. They actually wanted to have people that they might you know

shout and scream but at the end of the day would go along with them because they sort of, you know, they … it's, it's what they want is not to represent the community and challenge the police, what they want is to be represented across the community. And that was very clear and the police knew that. Very well. And I don't think it's just with the Muslim community. I've seen it being played out in the black community and so forth. Police have always chosen that avenue rather than facing real challenges.

At a workshop that I organised in Washington DC in June 2011, involving Muslim community members, police officers and researchers, a key theme that emerged from discussions around police and community engagement was that often there has been no engagement, where engagement is viewed as being about the overcoming of differences. At the same time, individuals spoke about how many Muslims have been treated as though they owe something to their host country, when many are second or third or later generation American. It was also stressed that whilst young Muslims may feel that they are being asked for their opinions, their ideas are being dismissed. Again, this highlights the importance of differentiating between real and superficial engagement.

In a later report, Innes et al. (2011) are concerned that whilst some mosques have been dealing with extremism, they have been doing so largely on their own, without involving the police. Moreover, in these cases the police are often not made aware of community interventions through the community contacts that they have. However, as highlighted in the previous chapter, it may be the case that for community members to act credibly with their key audiences it is essential for them to act independently, and this may mean independence from the police. This of course is a controversial point, but it does raise the question of what this means at a grassroots level in the co-production of security? Does this mean that at times it will be essential for community members to act without the knowledge of the police? For Innes et al. (2011: 42–3), the co-production of security is 'when local groups utilise public security resources to achieve an impact on a problem that neither could produce by their own means alone'. As demonstrated in chapter 2, co-production can actually mean community members delivering projects that police would like to deliver but are unable to due to their lack of credibility with communities. Therefore, co-production can mean community members taking the lead in programme implementation and delivery. It can also involve community members seeking unofficial, informal, advice from the police, as the following quotation from a police officer demonstrates:

> I went down to speak to the chairman of the mosque. I sat with him for an hour and a half. He knew who I was and why I was there and I could have been there a lot longer, to be honest, if I didn't have another meeting ... he phoned me up saying, 'We've got some issues. Could you possibly not officially deal with them but could you just give us some advice and come in and sort this out for us?' And that just took one meeting. I've only met him once.

Co-production can also involve partnership, an issue that Innes tends to overlook. Partnership in counter-terrorism has been promoted by Dr Robert Lambert, an ex counter-terrorism police officer who has written extensively about partnership approaches between police and communities and who set up the MCU.

Lambert (2008; 2010; 2011) has provided an 'insider account' of the work he engaged in with the MCU, reflecting on his practice-based experience. Lambert (2011) conceptualises the MCU as adopting a partnership approach, a partnership between a counter-terrorism policing unit and members of Muslim communities in London. The importance of understanding the local context to violent radicalisation is a theme that underpins the work of Lambert (2010) and indeed that of Baker (2010), both of whom write about the significance of locales for identifying specific vulnerabilities. Lambert (2010) focuses on examining two main case studies of partnership between police and communities at two mosques in London which experienced AQ-linked extremism during the 1990s – Brixton and Finsbury Park mosques. Lambert is keen to distinguish the partnership approach of the MCU from the informant-based culture traditionally operating in policing. Indeed, the following is a quotation from a Muslim community member who we interviewed, speaking about the distress created by the utilisation of an informant-based approach by police:

> IV:...one of our members was actually approached by MI6 and asked to co-operate as an informer and that was our very own committee members, so if they are approaching our bodies, you know ... it means that we may well be a suspect, because they have chosen us to try and recruit us. But we as a whole don't want to be considered as spies for the authorities, we want to retain an

independence from authority and show respect to them and we hope that we receive respect back.

Partnership is perhaps aptly conceptualised as 'equality, transparency and legitimate cooperation between partners, which may involve participants with different interests forming a partnership to carry out work that they collectively decide to do' (Spalek et al., 2009: 33). Partnership is challenging for police services, for police can have a tendency to control and manage partnerships. Moreover, in any partnership approach, it is likely that different partners will have different priorities and how these divergent sets of experiences and needs come together is a fascinating topic in itself. As a former practitioner, for Lambert (2011) it is important to develop an effective counter-terrorism policy, which means a policy that does not alienate the communities from which terrorists seek support and recruits. This is also stressed in academic literature (Schmid, 2004). For Lambert (2011), partnership offers such an approach:

> ... although informants were an important source of terrorist intelligence – just as they were for criminal intelligence – our experience suggested that community leaders and representatives were more likely to cooperate with police if they were treated as partners and not as informants. To be an informant, in our experience, was to risk losing credibility, legitimacy and effectiveness in the communities to which they belonged. In contrast, in our experience, that credibility, legitimacy and effectiveness could be safeguarded if community leaders or representatives engaged with police in a wholly transparent manner. (Lambert, 2011: 60)

For Lambert (2011), the notion of partnership is best understood according to three stages: approach, engagement and consolidation. Approach is the term used to cover initial meetings between MCU officers and community representatives at which the prospect of partnership was discussed. Lambert (2011) makes a clear distinction between the use of this term in relation to MCU, and the use of the term 'approach' more generally in policing. This is because 'approach' is often used in policing as the term to describe the procedures surrounding a first approach between an officer and a potential informant. For Lambert (2011), engagement is the period that follows an approach when the police and community partners engage together in a joint project. This is also about having productive dialogue without necessarily having productive partnership. Consolidation describes the period when police and community partners reflect on the work they have done together and look towards learning lessons from each other (Lambert, 2011). This approach has been coined 'Lambertism' within policy circles and has been both supported and criticised. Criticism comes from the fact that the MCU partnered with Salafi and Islamist community members in London, which have often been viewed as potential dangerous 'radicals' within security and other circles. For Lambert (2011), it is the very fact that these people have strong and consistent standpoints on theological and political issues that provides them with the necessary credibility, legitimacy and skills to influence individuals at risk of AQ propaganda towards non-violence. Thus:

> Of course, I do not seek to argue that many of the Muslim Londoners I worked with to counter al-Qaeda influence are not fierce opponents of Israel's policy towards Palestine. On the contrary it is part of my case that their credible opposition to Israel's Palestinian policy at times played a key role in countering al-Qaeda influence in local communities in Britain. (Lambert, 2011: 33)

For Lambert (2011), effective counter-terrorism policing must involve building trust and partnerships with key community members – connectors as identified in research by Spalek and McDonald (2011) – because AQ propagandists and recruiters are also in the business of building trust and nurturing networks within the same communities. Thus, 'the MCU identified sections of Muslim youth in London who were the targets for AQ propagandists and embarked on trust-building with Muslim community partners who, as outreach workers, were able to access Muslim youth and work with them' (Lambert, 2011: 60). Being able to access young people is an issue that resonates deeply with the research that I and my team have conducted and with the empirical data that we have collected. There seems to be a real mistrust amongst young people towards police officers and so it is crucial for police to work with people from within communities – outreach workers as identified by Lambert (2011) – who can reach out to young people. The following is a quotation from a young Muslim woman interviewed by my team who spoke about young people's relationships with the police:

> when it comes to the, okay the Muslim and the youth, I'd say, they have no respect for the police whatsoever. I notice that the people who are going in

partnership with the police are the elderly people and it's not filtering down to the younger people because they don't know what to do. You know, they kind of say, you must, I don't know, 50,000 was, there was a seminar for anti you know, anti violence, anti terrorism, we'll get someone to talk, they'll get an old sheikh who'll just rattle on a few, for the last few, ideas from the Koran, about peace. And you're going to get how many youths? You know, because they're not interested, it's the wrong approach. I think definitely groups like ours, the younger people, need to be involved and really need to work directly with the police ... actually getting down to the young people who are on the road. You know, young people who have just reverted and who are angry.

This woman stresses how young people do not have any respect for the police, are often not involved in partnerships with the police, and that young people do not necessary listen to their elders. The work by McDonald (2012) further highlights the importance of being able to access and to work with young people, for whom counter-terrorism policy has been felt most acutely. McDonald (2012) has argued that grassroots initiatives are succeeding in engaging young Muslims in order to empower and support them.

The issue of trust is a complex one and will be tackled in chapter 4. What is so remarkable is that within a post 9/11 context of distrust and fear between police and Muslim communities, the MCU was able to build relationships with members of Muslim communities (Spalek, 2010). Other key researchers within the counter-terrorism policing arena include Spalek, El-Awa and McDonald (2009), Ramirez (2008), Silk (2009) and Hanniman (2008). In the US, Ramirez (2008) has been at the forefront of research, policy and practice in relation to building bridges between Arab Muslim communities and the police within a counter-terrorism context. Ramirez (2008) has argued that whereas counter-terrorism has traditionally relied on the analysis of domestic and friendly foreign government intelligence rather than the engagement of communities and the development of partnerships between communities and local law enforcement agencies, more recently, there has been a movement towards the utilisation of community policing within a counter-terrorism context, with partnerships being developed between police and Muslim, Arab, Sikh and South Asian American communities (Ramirez, 2008). Nonetheless, significant obstacles to community policing in relation to counter-terrorism in the US remain. For a number of years now, police departments in the

US have been accused of infiltrating mosques and of approaching Arab Muslim citizens as informants rather than as partners (see Chapter 4 for more details). Similarly, in Canada, there has been a movement towards the adoption of community policing within the remit of national security policing. Hanniman (2008), a police officer himself, argues that since 9/11 Canada's Muslim population has experienced increased scrutiny of their communities, alongside rising Islamophobia. The Royal Canadian Mounted Police (RCMP) put together a National Security Community Outreach Program (NSCOP) to establish positive relations with all Canadian communities, including Muslim Canadians, to increase understanding and trust between the public and police organisations and to ensure that all Canadians are treated equally and effectively protected. A number of community outreach initiatives have been undertaken by the RCMP in order to increase public understanding of the RCMP's role in national security and to create greater openness and transparency in the RCMP's work and procedures (Hanniman, 2008). Hanniman (2008) argues that adopting a community policing approach to national security can be problematic since community policing programmes can be used to exploit relationships in order to penetrate communities for the purposes of gathering criminal intelligence. Hanniman (2008) therefore stresses that gaining criminal intelligence through the RCMP's outreach programme was not the intent. Rather, the RCMP's community interactions were to identify problems, to find solutions and to provide communities with reassurance – intelligence was seen as a secondary issue.

The importance of a focus on relationship-building rather than on obtaining community intelligence is stressed in the work of Silk (2009), Spalek et al. (2009), Spalek, (2010) and Spalek and McDonald (2011). Relationship-building has to be undertaken within a very challenging context in which individuals are being stopped and searched and questioned, particularly at airports. State counter-terrorism approaches continue to rely heavily on the use of profiling and surveillance systems, so where police officers are beginning to build relationships with communities in local contexts their relationships are likely to be influenced by the policies and practices of the broader counter-terrorism arena. The following is a quotation from a young male Muslim who we interviewd in relation to his being stopped and questioned at an airport:

Obviously the anti terrorism legislation at the moment is of key importance ... about three of four months ago I came back to an airport, City Airport, and you know there was the anti-terror kind of police there and me and a friend of mine as soon as we kind of came through this 'can we see your passports', and they said 'can you wait over there, keep your luggage?' And then they said to me 'can you come into this room?'

The young man speaks about how he was questioned, during this stop at the airport, on matters that are political:

And then the first question that the guy asked me is 'what are your views on Hamas?' you know, me, I work in this kind of political things and that, so I thought you know, okay, I said 'well actually that's quite a political question that you just asked me. I've just got off a plane. And the first thing you're asking me is that, can I have some solicitors with me?' He said to me 'you're not entitled to a solicitor'... his words were 'you have no rights, we have all the rights. You're not entitled to a solicitor, if you refuse to cooperate and answer our questions we can prosecute you because we're detaining you under ...' I think it was schedule 11 or something of the Terrorism Act.

He describes this approach as being 'heavy', especially as he had just got off from a flight from Prague:

And I thought, do you know what I mean, it's a bit heavy and a bit much when, you know, you've just got off a plane, you know, coming back from Prague and that's what I'm having to go through. And then it was two hours of interrogation of all kinds of questions, you know, what are my views on Al Qaeda? What do I think of suicide bombing? What do I think of British soldiers getting killed in, you know, Afghanistan and Iraq? ... I can imagine for lots of people that must be quite a terrifying experience. Do you know what I mean, you come off the plane and the next thing, and you know it's happened to lots of people that I know. It's not just a random list, it's lots of people.

Being stopped at the airport and being questioned in this way has obviously had a deep impact on this young man. Any community police officers wishing to build a relationship with him would need to understand his particular set of grievances.

The following is a quotation from a young Muslim woman talking about the strained relationship between herself and police:

the relationship from, in, in my, the way I see it is, is a relationship of hatred.

There's no respect and I must admit even me personally, I'd walk past and see a policeman, two plonkers, you know, because it's just the way, it's just the way you see things on a daily basis.

It appears that her relationship with the police is strained because she sees police officers harassing people and also because she herself has been followed by the police:

You see them harassing people. They've harassed me, you know, I've driven through Dulwich in a nice car, I had a cap on, it was early in the morning, was driving through, and they started following me, I think they thought I was a boy. Erm, because all they saw was a cap and they, and I was driving a BMW, going through. They followed me all the way to Brixton from Dulwich. So I stopped the car, they didn't put their lights or anything, they just followed me. I stopped the car, one of them came round, Miss X? I said yes. Oh, okay, we were just checking. I said checking what? Er, we were just ... we don't mean to stop you, our lights shouldn't have been on, the lights weren't even on, so he's just started stuttering, going on, he didn't have anything to say, they just didn't have anything to do, the car wasn't stolen, they could have checked to see if it was insured by just calling in the licence plate which they did because they called me by my name.

Interestingly, at a workshop that I ran involving police and communities in Belfast, Northern Ireland, in April 2011, police officers were talking about how policing is a very reactive job – responding to intelligence – and so within this context it is difficult to engage and to build relationships with communities. The Connect Project was highlighted as a good exampleof police officers and communities coming together outside of a crisis event in an environment of learning. Under the Connect Project police officers and community members were asked to talk about their experiences with each other, both good and bad. This was seen as a useful undertaking, serving to humanise police and community relations. At the same time, police officers expressed the real need for a covert style of policing, and that communities cannot expect 'hard' policing tactics to be removed for the sake of relationship-building. It was stressed here that what is key is accountability and oversight of any tactics and procedures that are applied. It was also highlighted that single interactions between police and community members often define how the police are perceived, and that every interaction leaves a trace; it requires fourteen good incidents to counteract one negative one. At this workshop it was also stressed by police officers that they can be nervous about walking in certain areas of Belfast due to concerns for their own safety, and the question was raised of what communities are doing about this. It was stressed by police that it is important for the community to understand police perspectives.

The critical importance of relationship building for community policing in relation to counter-terrorism cannot be stressed enough. The following is a quotation taken from an interview with a counter-terrorism police officer, who speaks about the importance of taking the time to build a relationship with communities, especially in the highly sensitised area of counter-terrorism:

> It literally is stopping people turning from those thoughts they have into a delib-
> erate act that's going to harm themselves, others, you know, it's really practical
> stuff. You know, stop them converting themselves into a terrorist. Or influ-
> encing others to do that. And then all the other work around that, the project
> work, building up good relations with the community, is contributing to that.
> Because it's recognised, and we recognised it quite early on that we just can't
> turn up at a Community Centre, a community, a Mosque, and go 'we're here
> from the Preventing Violent Extremism wing of the Counter Terrorism Unit,
> you know, let's be friends and let's stop it happening'. First of all there has to be
> a relationship. And I think we've probably learnt that a little bit quicker than the
> people who are deciding on policy and what's right.

However, it is important to highlight that relationship-building in a counter-terrorism context presents particular challenges, and therefore requires added sensitivity. In Britain, within the context of neighbourhood policing, police officers have dual responsibility for responding to ordinary crimes and also for policing violent extremism. There is a danger of community policing being co-opted into intelligence-led, covert, policing under the auspices of the neighbourhood policing model. Thus, there is a danger that neighbourhood policing is used as a means of developing trust between community members and police officers and this trust then being exploited as part of wider intelligence-gathering mechanisms, rather than being nurtured and built on to enable long-term partnerships to develop between police and community members. The incusion in the everyday activities of neighbourhood police officers of the prevention of violent extremism contains the risk that trust between communities and police will be eroded. This is because counter-terrorism is an arena traditionally dominated by covert rather than overt policing models, and so communities may be sceptical of any interest shown in them by neighbourhood police officers in relation to issues of violent extremism. At the workshop in Belfast mentioned above, community members spoke about how they did not want counter-terrorism to dominate the community safety agenda, and did not want a counter-insurgency agenda to pollute all the good work being done. It was also highlighted that communities have to be responsible for speaking out against violence against police officers. It was pointed out that whereas people are saying publically that covert policing is a problem, privately they are saying that it is overt counter-terrorism policing that is problematic. It seems that communities themselves are unclear about what they want from policing, and so naturally police do not know how communities want them to respond.

A study by Spalek and McDonald (2011) exploring police and community engagement within a counter-terrorism context highlights how the police officers who were interviewed said they spent a considerable amount of time trying to convince community members that they are not interested in spying on people and are not part of any surveillance mechanisms, but are trying to clarify where the boundaries should be placed in terms of what information should come to the attention of the police. Due to the sensitivities involved in overt counter-terrorism policing models, it is therefore important for police officers to be reflexive practitioners, and to show sensitivity and delicacy in the approaches they make to community members. It is the lack of delicacy and the focus on obtaining intelligence that has been criticised by Kundnani (2009), in an influential report called *Spooked! How Not To Prevent Violent Extremism*. This report was based on an exploration of the Prevent strategy in Britain. The study on which the report was based involved a total of 32 interviews with Prevent programme workers and managers in local authorities, with voluntary sector workers engaged in Prevent work, and with community workers familiar with local Prevent work. The evidence that emerged was controversial and gained much publicity. Kundnani's (2009) report contained some key criticisms of Prevent. Kundnani (2009) argued that a significant part of Prevent involved embedding counter-terrorism police officers in the delivery of local services with the apparent purpose of gathering intelligence, as well as managing perceptions and grievances. Furthermore, voluntary sector and local authority workers are increasingly suspicious of the expectations placed on them to provide information to the police. Prevent has been targeted at Muslims, and there is a perceived atmosphere that to make any radical criticisms of government is to risk losing funding, which undermines channels for effective and open discussions with young people who may be influenced by ideologies that legitimate illegitimate political violence (Kundnani, 2009). For Kundnani (2009), the Prevent agenda is the depoliticisation of Muslim communities. Moreover, for Kundnani (2009: 6), 'Prevent decision-making lacks transparency and accountability. Decisions are taken behind closed doors rather than in consultation with the voluntary and community sector'. Below is a quotation from a young male Muslim that my team and I interviewed in relation to the Prevent agenda. Echoing some of the criticisms presented by Kundnani (2009), he talks about the pressures being placed on certain individuals in Muslim communities to embrace Prevent:

> Absolutely. If you apply pressure which there's a lot of pressure on the Muslim community, but I wouldn't say the pressure is on all of the Muslim community, because that would be disingenuous, because pressure isn't on all of the Muslim community. It's on certain elements within a local community. So the gatekeepers are under pressure to join the programme and to work toward the objectives of the programme. Because most of the community doesn't matter. You only need the key people in the community and key leader networks or KLMs or whatever they're called, you only need those and they will then relay that message to the relevant sectors of that local community.

He continues by arguing that the state has co-opted those individuals within Muslim communities through whom the Prevent agenda and counter-terrorism policy can be implemented:

> When it comes to the state responding to ... security or threats to its national security, it only applies pressure on those that it needs to apply pressure on. And they're then co-opted and they then forward on the relevant messages or the relevant narrative to those members of the community that aren't necessarily involved. So pressure is applied indirectly through the Muslim community onto the Muslim community.

He then speaks about the importance of gatekeepers within the Muslim community, and how government policy can be forced onto a community through the gatekeepers:

Or through the gatekeepers of the Muslim community through to the lower level of the community ... So what we need to do is we need to understand the relationship between the gatekeepers and everybody else within the community, and how these two communicate and respond ... Nobody gets to ... briefings, the gatekeeper gets briefings and the briefings are handed out. So if we understood how that pressure from the state was being channelled to the local community via the gatekeepers, it would allow us to understand how the policy is being spread onto the local level. Also it's very important to research who these so called gatekeepers are. Who made them gatekeepers? Why are they considered to be gatekeepers? Why are they so influential? I think it's very important to understand this.

The above quotation is interesting, given that in the previous chapter I have argued that for those individuals engaged in counter-terrorism as conflict transformation credibility is key. Credibility is about challenging state-led agendas where these are perceived to be unjust. Therefore, a key question for future research is what are the ways in which members of communities may be co-opted into state-driven security agendas, and in what ways might some individuals challenge such agendas.

The above paragraphs have summarised some of the key arguments and positions articulated by some of the leading and high-profile voices regarding community policing and counter-terrorism post 9/11. With the exception perhaps of Kundnani (2009), all of these authors are generally supportive of a more overt approach in counter-terrorism and adopting a localised approach that includes community policing. A key distinction between the work of Innes and that of Lambert, Spalek, Ramirez, Hanniman and Silk is perhaps the emphasis placed upon community intelligence as opposed to relationship building and providing community reassurance. Underpinning Innes' (2006) approach is this notion of 'soft power', whereby strategic engagement is for police to be able to challenge rumours that circulate within communities, and also for engagement to act as an intelligence feed for police. This focus on police and community engagement for intelligence purposes could be accused of exploiting relationships and networks for intelligence gathering purposes. In a counter-terrorism context where criminality and the nature of intelligence is much more diffuse and ill-defined than for ordinary crime, this can be deeply problematic. This emphasis on intelligence is very concerning, given the apparent level of mistrust and the lack of confidence regarding counter-terrorism policing within

Muslim communities (Spalek, 2010). The work by Lambert, Spalek, Ramirez, Hanniman and Silk stresses 'soft engagement', and the use of 'soft' policing skills in relation to dialogue, relationship-building, trust-building, but also highlights that intelligence should not be the key, or even a focus, for community policing. Rather, police and community engagement should be about providing communities with reassurance, particularly as Muslim communities have been experiencing substantial and heightened Islamophobia since 9/11 (Lambert and Githens-Mazer, 2010). The work of Lambert, Spalek, Ramirez, Hanniman and Silk has included highlighting a skill-set for police that includes cultural and emotional intelligence, human connection, being able to elicit trust, and so forth. However, this body of work has largely been ignored by policy makers and key decision-makers within policing, and any contribution that Lambert has made has been largely overlooked as a result of the engagement of the MCU with 'radicals'.

There is of course an argument that community policing skills and strategies should not be employed within counter-terrorism, for this is too much of a blurring between police services and the security services (Thiel, 2009). The security services also use 'soft tactics' in relation to relationship-building, trust-building, cultural and emotional intelligence and even disruption tactics like knocking on someone's door to show that they are under state scrutiny. Should skills and experiences developed within a covert security context be transferred to a policing context? The following is a quotation taken from an interview that we conducted with a police officer that serves to illustrate a focus on 'disruption' tactics by counter-terrorism police officers:

> So that balance, so actually we've got intelligence to say that they could be about to do something, when do we jump? So it's a disruption. We might not get a conviction, but we've potentially stopped an atrocity ... And it's sometimes a very subjective decision where you have very little intelligence around it and you're balancing, well, if something goes boom and we knew ... so do I stop the chance of something going boom, but we've then disrupted and not convicted a network. So those type of things go on. It is complex and sometimes perhaps those people, their behaviour may be suspicious but there's nothing illegal that they're doing.

In many ways, 'softer' skills that feature in more covert, security-led approaches have already been applied within overt counter-terrorism policing contexts.

Could this decrease the legitimacy of the police, particularly when this is often based on accountability and the rule of law being seen to be upheld and equal for all citizens (Huq, Tyler and Schulhofer, 2011)? Or, on the contrary, by increasing the scope of 'soft' security-related skills within community policing approaches to counter-terrorism, might a better balance be attained between overt and covert approaches? Work traditionally carried out by the security services might be transferred to more overt policing approaches which may play an important role in deterring terrorism. This raises the question of what members of the public generally, and of Muslim and other securitised communities more specifically, might perceive the legitimacy of such policing tactics to be. Where there is little perceived legitimacy for such tactics it may be that their adoption will add to, rather than reduce, conflict between police and communities. This is an ongoing and real issue for counter-terrorism and counter-terrorism policing, one that is insufficiently researched and understood.

Conclusion

This chapter has focussed upon some of the key debates and research in relation to counter-terrorism policing, specifically post 9/11. Whilst there has been a substantial interest in active or passive support for terrorism amongst communities, the almost exclusive focus upon Muslim communities contributes to their stigmatisation and securitisation. At the same time, the focus on active or passive support for terrorism amongst Muslims often fails to consider the social and political factors that underpin any such support, factors such as poverty or disenfranchisement. Localism appears to be a common theme in the literature, particularly in the work by Professor Innes and his colleagues. However, this focus on local dynamics and local griev-ances may be problematic in that it does not take wider factors sufficiently into consideration, and thus represents a de-politicisation of the issues at stake. Local grievances, local factors, may have their roots in interna-tional dynamics, in geo-political power plays involving nation-states. Innes' approach potentially places police officers within an overly-narrow lens, an overly naive position that can perhaps put police community relations under greater strain. This chapter also highlights the importance of police and communities engaging with each other than during a crisis event, as this can serve to humanise police and community relations. It is important, though to highlight that there can be major differences in perceptions between police officers and communities. Thus, police officers may express the need for a covert style of counter-terrorism policing, and feel communities cannot expect 'hard' policing tactics to be removed for the sake of relationship-building, even though communities argue that they dislike the use of tactics like surveillance, stop-and-search and informant-based approaches. It is also important to consider police officers' perceptions that they feel unsafe walking in certain neighbourhoods or areas and so what responsibility do community members have here in ensuring the safety of officers ? Another question raised in this chapter concerns the ways in which members of communities might be co-opted into state-driven security agendas, and the ways in which some individuals might challenge such agendas? Furthermore, could the application of 'softer' skills that feature in more covert, security-service led approaches within overt counter-terrorism policing contexts decrease the legitimacy of the police, particularly when legitimacy towards policing is often based on accountability and the rule of law being seen to be upheld and equal for all citizens? Or by increasing the scope of 'soft' security-related skills within community policing approaches to counter-terrorism might a better balance between overt and covert approaches be achieved? What might the perceived legitimacy of such policing tactics be among members of the public generally, and among members of Muslim and other securitised communities specifically? The next chapter considers citizenship, the acceptance of responsiblity and trust in relation to counter-terrorism as conflict transformation. The chapter considers how states can encourage and actively persuade citizens to work within state-driven counter-terrorism agendas in a context of differentiated citizenship where there may be competing loyalties associated with experiences of belonging at a global, as well as national and local level .

Bibliography

Anderson, E. G. (2011) 'A Dynamic Model of Counterinsurgency Policy Including the Effects of Intelligence, Public Security, Popular Support, and Insurgent Experience', *System Dynamics Review* 27: 111–41.

Baker, A. (2010) *Countering Extremism in the UK: A Convert Community Perspective.* PhD thesis, University of Exeter.

Chavez, T. (2012) *Perspectives on Community Policing: A Social Constructivist and Comparative Analysis.* Unpublished PhD Thesis, University of Birmingham.

Crenshaw, M. (1981) 'The Causes of Terrorism'. *Comparative Politics* 13(4), 379–99.

Hanniman, W. (2008) 'Canadian Muslims, Islamophobia and National Security Royal Canadian Mounted Police'. *International Journal of Law, Crime and Justice,* 36(4): 271–85.

Huq, A., Tyler, T. and Schulhofer, S. (2011) 'Mechanisms for Eliciting Co-operation in Counter-terrorism Policing'. Public Law and Legal Theory Research Paper Series Paper No. 340, The Law School, University of Chicago. Available at: http://papers.ssrn.com/sol3/papers.cfm?abstract_id=1757266# (accessed 5 April 20013).

Innes, M. (2006) 'Policing Uncertainty: Countering Terror through Community Intelligence and Democratic Policing'. *Annals of APSS,* 605: 1–20.

Innes, M., Abbott, L., Lowe, T. and Roberts, C. (2007) *Hearts and Minds and Eyes and Ears: Reducing Radicalisation Risks Through Reassurance Oriented Policing.* Cardiff: Cardiff University.

Innes, M., Innes, T. and Roberts, C. with T. Lowe and S. Lakhani (2011) *Assessing the Effects of Prevent Policing: A Report to the Association of Chief Police Officers Universities.* Police Science Institute Cardiff: Cardiff University.

Kundnani, A. (2009) *Spooked! How Not to Prevent Violent Extremism.* London: Institute of Race Relations.

Lambert, R. (2011) *Countering Al Qaeda in London: police and muslim partnerships* London: Hurst & Company.

Lambert, R. and Githens-Mazer, J. (2010) *Islamophobia and Anti-Muslim Hate Crime.* London: European Muslim Research Centre. McDonald, L. Z. (2012) 'Engaging Young People within a Counter-Terrorism Context' in: B. Spalek (ed.) Counter-Terrorism: community-based approaches to terror crime Basingstoke: Palgrave MacMillan pp. 90–136.

Moore, S. (2012) 'Breivik's Ideology is All Too Familiar: That's Our Big Problem'. *The Guardian,* Wednesday 18 April, http://www.guardian.co.uk/commentisfree/2012/apr/18/breiviks-ideology-is-all-too-familiar?intcmp=239 (accessed 23 April 2012).

Ramirez, D. (2008) 'Partnering for Prevention', http://www.northeastern.edu/law/academics/institutes/pfp/index.html (accessed 6 January 2012).

Rowe, M. (2004a) *Policing, race and racism.* Cullompton: Willan Publishing.

—(2004b) 'Frameworks for Conceptualising Terrorism'. *Terrorism and Political Violence*, 16(2): 197–221.

Schmid, A. (2007) 'Terrorism and Democracy', *Terrorism and Political Violence* 10(3): 14–25.

Silk, D. (2009) 'Outreach between Muslim Communities and Police in the UK: Preliminary Report'. University of Birmingham.

Spalek, B. (2010) 'Community Policing, Trust and Muslim Communities in Relation to "New Terrorism"'. *Politics & Policy* 38(4): 789–815.

Spalek, B., El-Awa, S. and McDonald, L. Z. (2009) 'Engagement and Partnership Work in a Counter-Terrorism Context' University of Birmingham.

Spalek, B. and McDonald, L. Z. (2010) 'Anti-Social Behaviour Powers and the Policing of Security' *Social Policy and Society* Vol. 9 (1) pp. 123–33.

—(2011) 'Preventing Religio-Political Violent Extremism Amongst Muslim Youth: a study exploring police-community partnership' University of Birmingham.

Thiel, D. (2009) *Policing Terrorism: A Review of the Evidence.* London: Police Foundation.

WMPA (2008) 'Preventing Violent Extremism – Communities and Local Government Committee', http://www.publications.parliament.uk/pa/cm200910/cmselect/cmcomloc/65/65we01.htm (accessed 16 December 2011).

Young, J. (1999) *The Exclusive Society.* London: Sage.

4

Citizenship, Responsibilisation and Trust in Counter-Terrorism

Introduction

As demonstrated in the previous chapters, the causes of terrorism are contested, as are understandings of appropriate response and prevention strategies. Between nation states there exist competing claims over truth, which are largely linked to geo-political power plays. Within and between communities there also exist competing narratives about issues such as the legitimacy of terrorist acts, the proportionality or not of responses to terrorism, the dangerousness of 'radicalisation', the importance of social and economic factors in understanding violent extremism, and so forth. Of significance within the context of such a contested terrain, in many western nation-states including Britain, the US, Canada and Australia, counter-terrorism policy includes a large focus on active citizenship. Individuals as citizens are expected to act responsibly in the face of threats from terrorism, spotting signs of vulnerability within their family, work and other cohorts, and informing appropriate authorities. Individuals as members of communities are also expected to engage with the state in order to prevent terrorism – as argued by Briggs et al. in 2006, the notion that 'communities can defeat terrorism' has become a popular counter-terrorism maxim. As in other areas of social policy – crime, health, welfare – individuals are being viewed as an important resource for preventing terrorism, as part of their responsibilities as active citizens and as members of wider communities. This focus on active citizenship within counter-terrorism policy constitutes a radical shift from traditional counter-terrorism policies and practices. States are attempting to engage, and even build partnerships, with individual citizens and with the wider communities that they belong to, rather than automatically drawing upon 'hard' counter-terrorism tactics that involve the use of informants, surveillance and so forth.

Whilst at an abstract level, citizenship refers to legal, political and social equality (Marshall, 1950), in practice, even within liberal democratic systems, citizenship is differentiated, and there are often significant inequalities between individual citizens and between the wider group collectivities that they belong to (Spalek, 2008). In the context of security, there are many historical and contemporary examples of individual citizens, and the wider communities to which they belong, experiencing differentiated state-led approaches. In the context of Northern Ireland, for example, Irish Catholic citizens in particular experienced differentiated citizenship by being 'suspect communities' and thereby more likely to be experiencing 'hard' counter-terrorism responses (Hillyard, 1993). Post 9/11, Muslim communities have experienced differentiated citizenship as a result of their securitisation and, increasingly, their responsibilisation – being viewed as the moral agents of terrorism prevention initiatives (Choudhury and Fenwick, 2011; Spalek and McDonald, 2011), even though threats from terrorism are multifaceted, involving separatist, left-wing and anarchic, alongside Islamist, groups.

Whilst there is a substantial amount of research literature about the securitisation of particular communities and their experiences of 'hard-edged' counter-terrorism policies and practices (Pantazis and Pemberton, 2009; Spalek, El-Awa and McDonald, 2009; Kundnani, 2009; McGovern, 2010; Hickman and Silvestri, 2011; Choudhury and Fenwick, 2011), there is much less analysis and understanding of individuals' engagement with 'softer' counter-terrorism policies and practices, at the core of which lies the notion of active citizenship. What is less clear, therefore, is the issue of how states can encourage and actively persuade citizens to work within state-driven counter-terrorism agendas in a context of differentiated citizenship where there may be competing loyalties associated experiences of belonging at a global, as well as national and local level. In the post 9/11 context, for example, what challenges are there for policy makers attempting to involve and engage with members of Muslim communities for counter-terrorism purposes? This is a question that I and my team have been researching for a number of years now in the context of counter-terrorism policy and practice in Britain in relation to Al Qaeda (AQ) linked terrorism. A key theme that keeps recurring in many of the interviews that we have undertaken is that of the notion of trust. Interviews with police officers, probation officers, youth workers, community members and others indicate the importance of trust for 'softer' counter-terrorism policies. It seems that trust enables state and non-state actors to negotiate spaces of engagement and even partnership within the complex counter-terrorism terrain. This suggests that underpinning 'softer' counter-terrorism policies and practices are themes that resonate more directly with conflict transformation – the ability of state and non-state actors to work through any incompatibilities and struggles they may have, with trust serving as the social glue for this. This chapter focuses predominantly on the issue of trust, for this is often a neglected area in research relating to preventing terrorism. The chapter draws on interview data in order to shed light upon questions relating to what trust is, how it is built, and what its significance is for counter-terrorism as conflict transformation. First the key themes of community resilience, active citizenship, trust and confidence in policing will be discussed, before interview data about trust and counter-terrorism as conflict transformation is presented and analysed.

Counter-terrorism policies, community resilience and active citizenship

In Britain, the notion of community resilience features significantly in 'softer', community-based approaches to counter-terrorism. For example, in 2006, a Commission on Integration and Cohesion was announced, which was to consider how local areas themselves could play a role in forging cohesive and resilient communities by 'examining the issues that raise tensions between different groups in different areas, and that lead to segregation and conflict; suggesting how local community and political leadership can push further against perceived barriers to cohesion and integration; looking at how local communities themselves can be empowered to tackle extremist ideologies; and developing approaches that build local areas' own capacity to prevent problems, and ensure they have the structures in place to recover from periods of tension' (Commission on Integration and Cohesion, 2006). In the Department for Communities and Local Government (DCLG, 2007) document *Preventing Violent Extremism – Winning Hearts and Minds*, it is stated that 'key to this must be the building of strong communities, confident in themselves, open to others, and resilient to violent extremism' (DCLG, 2007: 4). In the Review of the Prevent Strategy in 2011 the following phrases in relation to highlighting the significance of resilience can be found: 'vulnerability to violent extremism includes a lack of resilience in some places and communities' (Home Office, 2011: 18); 'resilience in the context of this document means the capability of people, groups and communities to rebut and reject proponents of terrorism and the ideology they promote' (Home Office: 2011: 108); 'a stronger sense of 'belonging' and citizenship makes communities more resilient to terrorist ideology and propagandists. We believe that Prevent depends on integration, democratic participation and a strong interfaith dialogue' (Home Office, 2011: 27).

Community resilience also features significantly in the Australian Counter-Terrorism White Paper (2010: iii) where it is one of the four key elements of the strategy, where resilience is to mean 'building a strong and resilient Australian community to resist the development of any form of violent extremism and terrorism on the home front'. According to the Australian Counter-Terrorism White Paper (2010: iv):

> Australia's counter-terrorism efforts are supported by our open democratic society. There are inherent strengths in our society that make Australia resilient to the divisive worldview of al-Qa'ida and like-minded groups. However, we know from experience that the terrorist narrative may resonate with a small number of Australians. It is incumbent upon all Australians to work together to reject ideologies that promote violence, no matter from where they arise or to what purpose they aspire. We must all support and protect the values and freedoms from which all Australians benefit. By reducing disadvantage, addressing real or perceived grievances and encouraging full participation in Australia's social and economic life, government policies can help to mitigate any marginalisation and radicalisation that may otherwise occur within the Australian community.

In the US counter-terrorism strategy, building a culture of resilience is a core guiding principle. It is stated that 'the United States and its partners are engaged in the full range of cooperative CT activities—from intelligence sharing to joint training and operations and from countering radicalisation to pursuing community resilience programs' (The White House, 2011: 6). Furthermore, '... we will continue to assist, engage, and connect communities to increase their collective resilience abroad and at home' (The White House, 2011: 10).

The focus on resilience, and in particular community resilience, illustrates how important it is considered for individuals from within communities to be responsible and active citizens, to be moral agents and help prevent terrorism. This focus heralds a radical shift from traditional counter-terrorism policies and practices, which have pursued 'hard-ended' policies and practices involving surveillance and the use of informants amongst other tactics (Hewitt, 2010). The emphasis on communities and resilience perhaps reflects Durodie's (2005) observations that traditionally, whilst counter-terrorism policies have focussed on fostering technical resilience, insufficient emphasis has been placed upon fostering cultural resilience:

> Yet a political debate as to cultural values and social direction is noticeable by its absence. Instead, counter-terrorist measures put in place since 2001 can at best be described as technical in character. These include more surveillance, better intelligence, new protective clothing for so-called 'first responders', along with gadgets to detect chemical, biological or radiological agents, concrete blocks and fences around public buildings, endless checks at airports and stockpiles of vaccines. The problem with these is that, in seeking to secure society from the outside, we fail simultaneously to engage society from the inside with a view to winning a debate as to what we actually stand for.

According to Coafee (2008), developing community resilience is seen as potentially reinforcing institutional security strategies and as a way of mobilising citizens to pursue counter-terrorism goals. The focus on communities, citizens and resilience signals the responsibilisation of individual citizens, citizens being held responsible for being resilient against terrorism and violent extremism. With the focus still being very much on AQ-linked terrorism, despite a recent spate of far-right extremist activities across Europe, it is Muslim communities that have attracted most attention from policy makers and counter-terrorism practitioners, in Britain, Australia, the US, Canada and many parts of Western Europe. As argued by Spalek and Lambert (2007: 2), 'in a post 9/11 context, Muslims' responsibilities as active citizens are being increasingly framed by anti-terror measures which encourage internal community surveillance so that the responsible Muslim citizen is expected to work with the authorities to help reduce the risk of terrorism'. Debates and policies on wide-ranging issues, including multiculturalism, loyalty, faith, secularism, social cohesion, have, when applied to Muslim communities, increasingly involved the responsibilisation of Muslim communities for preventing terrorism. Therefore, questions of identity, and citizenship itself, have been co-opted into a wider security agenda that has potentially stigmatised Muslim communities (Spalek and McDonald, 2010).

At the same time, the focus on resilience, citizenship and communities within counter-terrorism policies and practices is indicative of a 'risk society' (Beck, 1992). Within a risk-based society, governments and state institutions are unable to manage the risks associated with modernity, and so there is increased emphasis upon an active citizenship that is self-regulating and able to mitigate modern-day risks. This reflects the imposition of a consumer culture within the public sector, an approach that the Conservatives brought into Britain under Prime Minister Margaret Thatcher and Prime Minister John Major, which was then continued by the subsequent Labour and Tory/Liberal Democrat governments of the late 1990s through to today. A risk-based approach to counter-terrorism also involves the state communicating risk to its citizens, and the ways in which this is done will have significant repercussions, either adding to or reducing fears (Mythen and Walklate, 2006). As mentioned previously, not all citizens are equal. Counter-terrorism policies and practices have focused predominantly upon Muslim communities, thereby singling them out as being especially responsible for preventing terrorism. The language of community resilience and citizenship presumes that all individuals have equal choice in deciding whether to help counter terrorism or not. However, in a post-9/11 world, Muslim minorities living within western democratic states have much less freedom and choice in relation to counter-terrorism initiatives, because many of these focus explicitly on Muslim communities. The ideal of 'active citizenship' also echoes the rise of the new criminologies (Garland, 1992: 458), which place responsibility for crime squarely onto individuals, as exemplified by the popularity of Professor Martin Innes' situational crime prevention approach to countering terrorism, discussed in chapter 3. Through the risk-based situational approach, significant differences in the structural positions that individuals occupy are left outside any prevailing discourse, and yet as highlighted in chapter 3, social and economic factors are not irrelevant when examining why individuals commit acts of terrorism (Schmid, 2007).

Within the national counter-terrorism strategies of western liberal states, there is some mention of the importance of taking into consideration real and perceived grievances in relation to preventing terrorism. In the original Prevent Strategy in Britain in 2007, and in the subsequent Prevent Review in 2011, it is acknowledged that real and imagined grievances can help drive AQ-linked radicalisation. Prevent is about addressing such grievances. In the Australian Counter-Terrorism White Paper (2010: 20) it is stated that 'by reducing disadvantage, addressing real or perceived grievances and encouraging full participation in Australia's social and economic life, government policies can help to mitigate any marginalisation and radicalisation that may otherwise occur within the Australian community'. In the US counter-terrorism strategy, the role of grievance is also given some attention:

> To rally individuals and groups to its cause, al-Qa'ida preys on local grievances and propagates a self-serving historical and political account. It draws on a distorted interpretation of Islam to justify the murder of Muslim and non-Muslim innocents. Countering this ideology—which has been rejected repeatedly and unequivocally by people of all faiths around the world—is an essential element of our strategy (The White House, 2011: 3).

Furthermore, it is stated that:

> Governments that are responsive to the needs of their citizens diminish the discontent of their people and the associated drivers and grievances that al-Qa'ida actively attempts to exploit (The White House, 2011: 5).

Grievance, trust and confidence in policing

The above discussion illustrates the importance placed upon the notion of grievance by national governments in their counter-terrorism strategies. Interestingly, counter-terrorism policing is not directly mentioned as a potential source of local grievance that terrorist strategists might exploit, yet it would appear that counter-terrorism policing is a key issue to consider when examining the significance of grievance in relation to counter-terrorism.

In Britain, secondary analysis of national crime survey data – the British Crime Survey – by Professor Innes and his team in a report commissioned by the Association of Chiefs of Police Officers (ACPO) in 2011 (*Assessing the Effects of Prevent Policing*) suggests that taken as a whole, Muslims in Wales and England hold higher levels of trust and confidence in police than the general population. It is through a secondary analysis of this data that Innes et al. conclude that counter-terrorism policing is not causing '*widespread or wholesale disengagement and disenchantment within Muslim communities*' (Innes et al., 2011: 54). This is seen as challenging an often-repeated view that Muslims have been alienated by counter-terrorism policing through the Prevent Strategy (Field, 2011b). It is important to note, however, that the use of quantitative data must be understood as a way of discerning broad trends within populations and that the complexities of populations are often not captured. Data pointing to the experiences of specific populations within specific locales is hard to gather quantitatively because large sample sizes are needed for quantitative analyses to be valid. This is time-consuming and resource-intensive work and so such data is often not gathered. Rather, experiences in relation to overarching categories like 'Asian', 'Black' or 'White' is often what is analysed within quantitative research (Spalek, 2008).

Returning to the specific issue of trust and confidence in policing amongst Muslim populations, national data-sets present 'average' Muslim community attitudes, and often obscure attitudinal differences amongst Muslims when taking into consideration factors such as age, religious sect, culture, gender and geographical location. There is a dearth of locally specific data in relation to local Muslim populations in Britain regarding issues of trust and confidence. According to Innes et al. (2011), Muslim young people have lower trust and confidence in their local police than do older Muslims. Moreover, less than half of young Muslim men (aged 16–24) gave the police a positive appraisal and this was lower than for men of the same age within the general population (Innes et al., 2011: 75). Innes et al. (2011: 75) use this analysis to argue that 'whilst there may be concerns about Prevent policing and it may impact moderately negatively on the views of some groups, there is not a strong anti-police position detectable in the mainstream Muslim population'. Innes et al. (2011: 6) conclude that 'whilst the "strong critique" of Prevent policing has achieved some political traction, the evidence collated suggests that it is not a mainstream or majority view within Muslim communities'. Importantly, however, if thinking about counter-terrorism policy and practice as responding to local grievances, then surely it is not mainstream or majority Muslim views that should necessarily be prioritised. Instead, there is great merit in focusing on the specific grievances of young Muslim men rather than being dismissive of these as 'minority perceptions', particularly as it is young Muslim, Arab and Asian men who are likely to bear the brunt of counter-terrorism strategies (Poynting and Mason, 2008).

Alongside young Muslim men as a specific population that needs further consideration in relation to trust and confidence in policing, there is also an argument for focusing on specific geographical locations. In Britain, a project by West Midlands Police called Project Champion generated substantial local and national criticism. In late 2007 West Midlands Police began creating a vehicle movement net involving CCTV cameras around two geographical areas within the city of Birmingham – Alum Rock and Sparkhill. The wider context for this was two significant terrorist plots in 2007, which had raised the national threat level to critical (Thornton, 2010). Two hundred surveillance cameras were placed in predominantly Muslim areas, some of which were hidden. The West Midlands Police Chief Constable is reported to have said that he was 'deeply sorry' that his force got the balance between counter-terrorism and excessive intrusion into people's lives 'so wrong'; and that, moreover, his real regret was that Project Champion had undermined the strong relationships that have existed between West Midlands Police and their communities (*The Telegraph*, 2010). The national outcry led to a review of Project Champion in 2010, conducted by Sara Thornton, Chief Constable of Thames Valley Police, which concluded that 'A proposal was made to establish a permanent surveillance capability in the area. While such a security ring exists in the City of London, this proposal was to create something similar in a semi-residential, predominantly Asian area. This thinking should have been challenged from the start and questions should have been asked about its proportionality, legitimacy, authority and necessity; and about the ethical values that underpinned the proposal' (Thornton, 2010: 48).

It would seem logical to suggest that it is important for research and policy in relation to trust and confidence in policing, and in counter-terrorism policing more specifically, to focus on specific locales – and in the Birmingham area in Britain this would mean a focus on the Alum Rock and Sparkhill areas. It would be important to access young Muslim men aged between 16 and 24 from within these locales in order to properly understand their grievances in relation to policing and counter-terrorism policing, to ensure that there is evidence-based policy and practice within these specific local areas. Currently, it appears that analyses of trust and confidence in policing with respect to Muslim, and indeed other, populations are rather too general, and that they obscure important specificities of experience. Gathering locally specific data about key groups of Muslims in relation to trust and confidence should be seen as a priority for police services that work in geographical areas where there are significant populations of Muslims, especially when it seems that the wider political and social context may be supportive of security approaches that focus on intelligence gathering and terrorism prevention initiatives being directed at Muslim populations. For example, according to Field (2011a), who looked at findings from a special '9/11 – ten years on' survey undertaken by YouGov on 6/7 September 2011, which involved an online sample of 1,947 adult Britons aged 18 and over, 63 per cent of adults wished to see Britain's security services focus their intelligence-gathering and terrorism-prevention efforts on Muslims living in or seeking to enter this country, on the grounds that, although most Muslims were not terrorists most terrorists threatening Britain were Muslim. It may therefore be that the police will be politically driven or influenced towards increasing or continuing their surveillance of Muslim communities, especially given that, since November 2012 there now are elected Police Commissioners in Britain for the first time.

Intelligence-gathering and surveillance approaches have a disproportionate impact on particular areas and groups of Muslims, and so as a priority, locally specific data is required, broken down according to ethnicity, age, religious sect, gender and so on. In the US, counter-terrorism policing has attracted criticism for its surveillance-based approach towards Muslim communities. The counter-terrorism tactics used by the New York Police Department (NYPD) in particular have attracted substantial criticism. Media reports highlight that the NYPD has adopted a pattern of surveillance and infiltration against American Muslims without any valid investigative justification. Media reports suggest that the NYPD infiltrated mosques, eavesdropped in cafes and monitored Muslim neighbourhoods with plainclothes officers (Associated

Press, 2012a). According to press reports, the 2006 NYPD intelligence report 'US-Iran Conflict: the threat to New York City' recommended increasing surveillance of Shia Muslims for tackling a perceived threat from Iranian terrorists (Associated Press, 2012b). According to a written statement to the US Senate Committee on the Judiciary Subcommittee on the Constitution, Civil Rights and Human Rights by the Council on American-Islamic Relations (CAIR):

> Since the tragic events of September 11, 2001, CAIR has received hundreds of reports from innocent Americans who have been wrongfully targeted by federal, state and local law enforcement officials because of their race, religion or national origin. They have been searched, investigated and detained without reasonable suspicion. Since then, the American Muslim community has become the unfair target of numerous federal and state counterterrorism initiatives and surveillance programs (CAIR, 2012: 2).

Understanding and directing policy attention towards issues of trust and confidence in policing amongst specific groups within Muslim communities should therefore be a key priority, especially given the responsibilisation of Muslims in relation to counter-terrorism policies. These discussions really highlight the challenges for community-based approaches to counter-terrorism, which increasingly hold the ideal of active citizenship at their core. The discussions above would suggest that not all citizens are equal with respect to the impacts of counter-terrorism strategies and, moreover, with respect to the responsibilisation towards preventing terrorism. Muslim communities in particular have borne the brunt of counter-terrorism policies, due, to some extent, to the focus of western states on AQ-linked terrorism.

The discussions above raise the question of whether it is possible to design counter-terrorism policies and practices that involve the notion of active citizenship. Can members of Muslim communities take a proactive civil stance towards national counter-terrorism strategies and work towards preventing terrorism? Or is it the case that the focus for all active citizens, not only for Muslims, should be a critique of state-driven counter-terrorism policies and practices where, despite state rhetoric around communities defeating terrorism and enhancing community resilience, in reality counter-terrorism continues to be largely driven by 'hard-edged' approaches that include surveillance and infiltration? Muslim community groups in particular have been faced with this dilemma: whether to partner and work with the authorities and/or to resist actively. 'Hard-edged' approaches raise civil liberties questions, for the disproportionate surveillance of Muslim communities would suggest racial and religious profiling, suggesting that not all citizens are equal before the law. Is it possible for non-state actors to implement nationally driven counter-terrorism policies in a way that is relevant to local contexts? Is it possible for non-state actors even to subvert those 'hard-edged' approaches that would appear to be so prevalent in counter-terrorism approaches? The next sections of this chapter draw upon data that has been gathered since 2007, from a wide range of state and non-state actors engaged in 'softer', community-based approaches to counter-terrorism that have active citizenship and community resilience at their core. The importance of trust is highlighted: it is this that enables state and non-state actors to negotiate spaces of engagement and even partnership within the complex counter-terrorism terrain. This suggests that underpinning 'softer' counter-terrorism policies and practices are themes that resonate more directly with conflict transformation – the ability of state and non-state actors to work through any incompatibilities and struggles they may have, with trust serving as the social glue for this.

Trust and trust-building

Whilst there is some literature on policing in relation to the notion of trust, there is little substantial analysis of trust-building between police and communities within sensitive, conflict-based, environments (Spalek, 2010). A substantial body of work indicates that trust in the police can be seriously undermined in situations where communities feel that they are being over-policed (Bowling and Phillips, 2007; Bridges and Gilroy, 1982; Hall et al., 1978; Jefferson, Walker, and Seneviratne, 1992; Jones and Newburn, 2001; Macpherson Inquiry, 1999; Sharp and Atherton, 2007; Sivanandan, 1981; Smith and Gray, 1985; Thacher, 2005; Waddington, Stenson, and Don, 2004). This is a significant issue, given that a number of commentators have highlighted the importance of trust for community intelligence. For example, according to Virta (2008, 30), 'trust and confidence towards the police is a precondition to community intelligence … It would be very difficult for the police to get community intelligence if people do not trust the police'. For Hillyard (1993, 2005), a breakdown of police-community relations can have serious consequences for policing, and in the context of counter-terrorism can halt the flow of vital information from communities. Innes et al. (2007) argue that low trust in the police can inhibit the willingness of individuals to pass community intelligence concerning a range of problems and issues, and a report by Demos (2007) highlights the importance of high trust relationships between communities and the police for effective national security in the age of 'home-grown terrorism'. A lack of community intelligence can lead to intrusive, 'hard' based policing strategies because suspicion tends to be of the community as a whole rather than being limited to specific groups or individuals .

Despite the importance of trust for community intelligence, little is known about how police officers and community members involved in 'soft' community-based approaches to counter-terrorism understand and experience trust, nor about the importance of the role of trust for them; whether trust is at all possible; whether there are different kinds of trust that can exist between police officers and communities; and the significance of this for community intelligence (Spalek, 2010). Interestingly, definitions of community policing have often left out trust, and yet an absence of trust can severely limit the development of community-police initiatives (Spalek, 2010). One suggested definition of community policing that I have previously put forward therefore contains the notion of trust:

> Community policing comprises community-oriented goals and objectives. It relies upon community consent in relation to policing initiatives and operations within communities. Trust between community members and police officers is an essential component of community policing (Spalek, 2010: 793).

Discussions around trust often focus upon the extent of any trust by community members in police officers. There is often an automatic assumption that trust is largely about communities trusting police rather than the other way around. The interview data I have gathered points to both sides of the equation really mattering – communities trusting police but also police officers trusting communities. Interview data points to the importance of police officers being open and honest with communities, as one police officer argued:

> I don't see how I could do the job that I'm doing if I wasn't honest and open and got trust ... Trust, it's just being open and honest so people know exactly where they stand with you.

The interview data highlights the importance of taking time to build trust, given the sensitivities that exist around preventing terrorism, as the following quotation from a counter-terrorism police officer illustrates:

> because you're talking about vulnerabilities and risk within their communities. And even though the community may feel, you know, they may know themselves that there is a risk within their communities, it's quite difficult for them to open up and admit that to police officers. But if they ... if you've spent time building up trust with them, you know, you get to that stage where you are able to have that difficult conversation with them because they trust you enough to have that conversation with you. And for me that's the real crux of it is do they trust you enough to discuss those difficult issues with you.

The importance of police officers taking the time to build trust with communities echoes the work by Goldsmith (2005), who has argued that trust is rooted in experience, in individuals' interactions with other people. It is crucial, however, to highlight that for police officers to build trust with community members it is often important for them to go beyond simply spending time and interacting with community members, and it may involve police officers actually demonstrating their trustworthiness, for example, by empowering communities to manage their sense of unease and uncertainty (Loader, 2006 in Spalek, 2010). The following is a quotation from a police officer talking about the steps s/he took to demonstrate her/his trustworthiness with a community member and with the wider community, by providing a number of initiatives as responses to racial incidents that took place which had not been reported officially to the police:

> ... a couple of community members, Somali community members, from the XXX Estate, came to us with, there was some racial incidents taking place which they hadn't reported, they didn't feel confident reporting, but within the Somali community, that was having quite a wide impact on how, how safe they felt and how they felt they integrated into the local community. Now we built trust with the community by basically dealing with that matter. And that wasn't just one thing, it was a number of things. That was reassurance patrols, it was talking to the families, it was interventions, it was working alongside the CID,

you know, making sure in the first instance that those instances were reported properly and then actioned properly. And then making sure that they knew we were there to do, you know, the whole safe neighbourhood piece ... and then I hope what that did, I'm pretty confident what that did is it showed them that they did have a voice within the local area and that they could speak up and say 'well actually this isn't right, we're not being treated very well here'. And address their grievances.

The following is a quotation from a community member showing how important it is for police and communities to demonstrate to each other that they are trustworthy through showing their 'competences' and 'results':

trust, the police service have had to trust us and have had to see our compe-tences and our, our results, our activities. And we also have had to trust them as well and, and see some of their, you know, what they've done. And so now at least these thing can come to, you know, they can come to an eventual end, whether it's been achieved or it hasn't been achieved and then we can go back to the community and say "you know what? There's no point in engaging with them because they never do anything." Because look, this is it. We've got evidence. These are our minutes, these are our activities, and this is what they have said. So I think this is positive and this accountability and this partner ... and this is where the partnership is. (Muslim Community Member in Spalek, 2010: 802)

One senior police officer argued that police have no right to ask for infor-mation, but rather, that it is important for them to engage with communities first, to develop a relationship based on trust and confidence and then an exchange of information may develop:

most importantly recognising that we have no rights to go into communities and ask for information, what we were saying to them was you must first engage and develop a relationship based on trust and confidence and then we believe that information will flow naturally.

It may be that police officers need to build contingent trust with community members before being able to hold relationships with community members that involve implicit trust. According to Goldsmith (2005), contingent trust is about building trust through being engaged in trust-building activities and through actors demonstrating their trustworthiness. Contingent trust is likely to be instrumental in that it looks at shorter-term rather than longer-term objectives and seeks confirmation through exchange relations. Contingent trust can later become implicit trust, which is a more advanced type of trust that can be found in committed, stable relationships (Goldsmith, 2005). Importantly, contingent and implicit trust applies equally to communities and police officers. Thus, it may be just as important for police officers to trust community members as it is for community members to trust police. Whilst some of the empirical data that I have gathered demonstrates that implicit trust can be built between police officers and community members, it is not necessarily the case that all police officers and all community members should seek to build implicit trust with each other. Implicit trust is perhaps most important for counter-terrorism initiatives that are based on partnership, involving community members as active citizens, actively working with specific police officers or policing units, engaged in deeply sensitive and risk-laden work. This may involve responding to gang violence and hate crime, alongside violent extremism. It may be that police involvement at too early a stage within such sensitive contexts could mean the loss of credibility for community members, who prefer first to appropriately challenge and prevent violence themselves before seeking help from the police:

> It's high risk, that is very, very high risk. There's been incidents where you know if it doesn't go the right way someone's getting killed. There's people armed in front of you. But if you don't deal with it in that way, these individuals, you'll lose their trust, their confidence, and they will go to extremists. (Muslim Community Member in Spalek, 2010: 804)

The reality on the ground in deprived urban areas where there is gang violence is that it is impossible for police to tackle this and other forms of extreme violence without the involvement of certain key community members. I would suggest that police and communities within these contexts have to have certain levels of implicit trust in each other in order to enable effective initiatives to be built. Informal social control will be undertaken by those community members with credibility, who, in attempting to prevent extreme forms of violence, may be putting themselves at risk. However, it is difficult to see how police officers can have the reach and effectiveness that community members may have in these challenging contexts, suggesting a significant reliance on community members to make risk-laden decisions:

An individual turns up in a big mackintosh because he had a dispute with another Muslim and the size of the weapon he had down the back of his coat and what did we do? Did we panic and run and call the police? We took him round the corner, my colleagues, spoke with him, really calmly. What are you doing? You're coming to a religious place, this is the house of God, it's a mosque. And you're coming to kill a Muslim? Do you know that killing a Muslim means that you go to the hellfire straight away? Eyes wide. Really? So if I killed this individual I will be punished? Yes you will. And even if he was wrong and he do this you'll still do this because you are not an authority to take anybody's life. What did he do? Jumped in the car, went home, put his weapon away, came back, made up with the individual. (Muslim Community Member in Spalek, 2010: 804)

The following quotation is from a police officer who argues that it is important for police not to view community members as suspects and to be able to put their trust in community members:

So from our perspective when you're dealing with say Salafi, you know, individuals and groups, you know, we just made a decision, you know ... I like you ... we seem to be working together really well. I need to put my trust in you first. Now ... you'll have been very well aware of the law enforcement establishments sort of putting the onus onto Muslim communities ... it's Muslim communities will sort this out, down to them, you know, so we'll support Muslim communities etc., but you know it really is down to them etc. And we're kind of saying well first of all we've got to put our trust in them. You know, so you can't just expect them just to get on with it, you know, you've got to work with them and you've got to trust them, so the trust that we're giving is ... you may as a community or as an organisation or an individual felt that you were somewhat marginalised or excluded from discussion or engagement around counter terrorism or Prevent, I want to turn that on its head now and say I really like you, I want to work with you and I want to trust you so I want you to do some of this and I'm going to tell you all about it.

This same police officer also speaks about the importance of telling community members about the work that he does and also giving community members access to information as a way of building trust:

And I'm going to tell you about me and what I do and I'm going to get you vetted so that you all of a sudden get access to a whole new world of information and activity that you haven't been trusted with or nobody has recognised that you can help us in the past. And does that come with some risk? Yes, it does. Yeah, it does, of course it does, but then there's no aspect of this work that doesn't come with some risk. And it's about, you know, making measured decisions that help to move this along.

Clearly, as demonstrated in the quotation above, in providing community members with access to information the police officer is taking some risk, however, he argues that this is a justified risk in terms of moving the relationship he has with communities along.

It is also important for police officers who are part of overt counter-terrorism units and approaches to be open and transparent about this. The Muslim Contact Unit, for example, which is a police unit in the Metropolitan Police Service that has applied community policing for counter-terrorism work, has involved police officers being open about them being counter-terrorism police officers, approaching community members as partners rather than informants (Spalek, 2010). MCU officers have argued that to be trusted by community members they have had to build up sincere relationships that are based upon being frank concerning the unit's remit. Without such honesty, the climate of fear generated by counter-terror laws and operations in Muslim communities can cause people to be distrustful of any approaches from police, particularly those that are not clearly defined (Spalek 2010). Research about the MCU would suggest that implicit trust is important not only for the effectiveness of sensitive community-based initiatives that tackle extreme forms of violence, but also because it can act as the glue that keeps police officers and community members partnering each other when external factors may impede more general police–community relations. Thus, international relations between nation states may influence British Muslim communities' perceptions of the British state, influencing their engagement with and perceptions of state actors, including the police. In a study by Spalek (2010), for instance, many Muslim participants spoke about how, from its conception, 'new terrorism' has been perceived by many as a war on Islam, causing reluctance within Muslim communities to help the police. So it would seem that within this very difficult political context, implicit trust can enable police and community members to engage in sensitive, community-based, preventative work in relation to extreme forms of violence: hate crime, gang violence and terrorism.

For more general engagement and outreach work, it is may be the case that police officers need to be clear about the boundaries of trust when interacting with community members, as the following quotation from a police officer illustrates:

> Trust is … it's them knowing that they can come to you with a problem and that you will deal with it to the best of your ability, but also acknowledging that there are boundaries, and those boundaries are in line with the role that we do and our, you know, our responsibilities as police officers, in that they know that … they know they can't just tell me something, you know if there's an offence there or I have an obligation to report back on that. They know that I will. So we're not talking about special favours, anything like that. But it's knowing that we will give the best advice and the best guidance and support that we possibly can within our role.

It is also important to consider the role of distrust in police and community interactions. Distrust is not necessarily a bad thing, as it can lead to more effective communication and engagement, as the following quotation from a community member illustrates:

> … no doubt there are police officers that are very trustworthy, they are you know, it would be wrong for me to say otherwise … but I think sometimes one feels that there's more of a motive, an exterior motive, for the police than meets the eye … to be honest with you on a few occasions they have been, well, I personally have said to a police, to senior officers, that I do not want to have any further interaction with him. Because I feel that he is gathering intelligence. So he's probably gathering intelligence behind me but now he's gathering it in front of me as well. So you know in asking questions, and getting other stuff.

The following community member stresses that young people in particular should not automatically be trusting, but that there should be sufficient trust in order to achieve core objectives:

> … I don't think young people should automatically think they have to trust everyone, I think there's a kind of healthy scepticism that young people need and that's part of their way of surviving. They shouldn't automatically trust the police in every aspect of what the police are doing or saying. There needs to be sufficient trust, that's the thing. If you've got sufficient trust you can work with that and achieve certain things, but I think there needs to be a healthy scepticism as well. And certainly a critical awareness of these very difficult complex issues.

Young, marginalised, people who may be engaged in drug taking and/or gang-related violence, although distrusting of police may trust the youth workers with whom they interact. Youth work provides these young people with safe spaces in which to discuss difficult issues, and youth workers can challenge viewpoints so as to avoid the escalation into violence which will involve the authorities. Youth workers can gain the trust of young people through long-term interaction and through experience (see McDonald, 2012 for further details).

Conclusion

This chapter focuses on citizenship, responsibilisation and trust, three inter-related dimensions to counter-terrorism as conflict transformation. It is highlighted that at the heart of 'softer', community-based strategies to counter-terrorism, is the notion of active citizenship – that individuals as citizens have a responsibility to help prevent terrorism. This chapter stresses that although citizenship at an abstract level implies equality, in reality individuals experience different levels of citizenship. When looking at citizenship in relation to nation-state security, particular communities have experienced differentiated state-led approaches to counter-terrorism. Post 9/11, Muslim communities have particularly experienced differentiated citizenship because they have borne the brunt of 'hard-edged' counter-terrorism policies and practices that have included detention without charge, surveillance and the use of informants. Indeed, in this chapter it is suggested that policing is a source of grievance, as a result of disproportionate 'hard' policing tactics targeted at Muslim communities. The question raised in this chapter is how, within a context of differentiated citizenship, states can encourage and actively persuade citizens to work within state-driven counter-terrorism policies. In the post-9/11 context, Muslim communities have undergone responsi-bilisation – they are viewed as the moral agents for terrorism prevention strategies. This then raises the question of what the challenges are for policy makers attempting to involve and engage with members of Muslim commu-nities for counter-terrorism purposes. Can members of Muslim communities take a proactive civil stance towards national counter-terrorism strategies and work towards preventing terrorism? Or is it the case that the focus for all active citizens, not only for Muslims, should be a critique of state-driven counter-terrorism policies and practices where, despite state rhetoric around communities defeating terrorism and enhancing community resilience, in reality counter-terrorism continues to be largely driven by 'hard-edged' approaches that include surveillance and infiltration? Muslim community groups have in particular been faced with the dilemma of whether to partner and work with the authorities and/or actively to resist.

This chapter demonstrates the complexities in a notion such as trust. There is often an assumption that trust is largely about communities trusting police rather than the other way around. The interview data I have gathered points to both sides of the equation really mattering – communities trusting police but also police officers trusting communities. The data presented in this chapter also highlights the importance of taking time to build trust, given the sensitivities that exist around preventing terrorism. Often, it is crucial for police officers and community members to go beyond simply spending time and interacting with each other, and actually demonstrating their trustworthiness through their competencies. It may also be that police officers need to build contingent trust with community members before being able to hold relationships with community members that involve implicit trust. According to Goldsmith (2005), contingent trust is about building trust through being engaged in trust-building activities and through actors demonstrating their trustworthiness. Contingent trust can later become implicit trust, which is a more advanced type of trust that can be found in committed, stable relationships (Goldsmith, 2005). This chapter also suggests that implicit trust is perhaps most important for counter-terrorism initiatives that are based on partnership, involving community members as active citizens, actively working with specific police officers or policing units, engaged in deeply sensitive and risk-laden work. This may involve responding to gang violence and hate crime, alongside violent extremism. It may be that police involvement at too early a stage within such sensitive contexts could mean the loss of credibility for community members, who prefer first to appropriately challenge and prevent violence themselves before seeking help from the police.

The next chapter focuses on two further dimensions that feature significantly in counter-terrorism policies: engagement and partnership.

Bibliography

Associated Press (2012) http://www.ap.org/Content/AP-In-The-News/2012/
    Document-shows-NYPD-eyed-Shiites-based-on-religion (accessed 11 May 2012).

Beck, U. (1992) *Risk Society: towards a new modernity* London: Sage.

Bowling, B. and Phillips, C. (2007) 'Disproportionate and Discriminatory: Reviewing
    the Evidence on Police Stop and Search' *Modern Law Review* 70 (6): 936–61.

Bridges, L. and Gilroy, P. (1982) 'Striking Back' (June): 34–5, http://www.
    amielandmelburn.org.uk/collections/mt/pdf/82-06-34.pdf (accessed 25 April
    2010).

Briggs, R., Fieschi, C. and Lownsbrough, H. (2006) 'Bringing it Home.
    Community-based approaches to counter-terrorism'. Demos, http://www.demos.
    co.uk/files/Bringing%20it%20Home%20-%20web.pdf (accessed 4 December
    2011).

CAIR (2012) *Written Statement of the Council on American-Islamic Relations on
    Ending Racial Profiling in America* submitted to the US Senate Committee on the
    Judiciary Subcommittee on the Constitution, Civil Rights and Human Rights,
    17 April 2012, http://www.cair.com/Portals/0/pdf/ERPAHearingTestimony.pdf
    (accessed 11 May 2012).

Choudhury, T. and Fenwick, H. (2011) *The Impact of Counter-Terrorism Measures on
    Muslim Communities.* London: Equality and Human Rights Commission.

Coaffee, J., Murkami-Wood, D. and Rogers, P. (2008) *The Everyday Resilience
    of the City: How Cities Respond to Terrorism and Disaster* Basingstoke:
    PalgraveMacMillan.

Commission on Integration and Cohesion (2006) *Our Shared Future* London:
    HMSO, http://resources.cohesioninstitute.org.uk/Publications/Documents/
    Document/DownloadDocumentsFile.aspx?recordId=18&file=PDFversion
    (accessed 3 April 2013).

Communities and Local Government (2007) *Preventing Violent Extremism – winning
    hearts and minds* London: Department for Communities and Local Government,
    http://resources.cohesioninstitute.org.uk/Publications/Documents/Document/
    DownloadDocumentsFile.aspx?recordId=133&file=PDFversion (accessed 3 April
    2013).

Demos (2007) *The Activist Police Force.* London: Demos.

Department of the Prime Minister and Cabinet (2010) *Counter-Terrorism White
    Paper – Securing Australia – Protecting Our Community* Canberra: Department of
    the Prime Minister and Cabinet, http://www.dpmc.gov.au/publications/counter_
    terrorism/ (accessed 3 April 2013).

Durodie, B. (2005) 'Terrorism and Community Resilience – A UK Perspective' Chatham House Briefing Paper ISP/NSC Briefing Paper 05/01, July 2005.

Field, C. (2011a) *British Religion in Numbers*, http://www.brin.ac.uk/news/2011/911-ten-years-on/ (accessed 5 April 2013).

—(2011b) *British Muslims and the Police*, http://www.brin.ac.uk/news/2011/british-muslims-and-the-police/ (accessed 5 April 2013).

Garland, D. (1992) 'Criminological Knowledge and its Relation to Power: Foucault's Genealogy and Criminology Today', Vol. 32 *British Journal of Criminology*, pp. 456–80.

Goldsmith, A. (2005) "Police Reform and the Problem of Trust." *Theoretical Criminology* 9 (4): 443–70.

Hall, S., Critcher, C., Jefferson, T., Clarke, J. and Roberts, B. (1978) *Policing the Crisis: Mugging, the State, and Law and Order*. London: Macmillan.

Hewitt, S. (2010) *Snitch! A History of the Modern Intelligence Informer*. London: Continuum.

Hickman, M., Silvestri, S. and Nickels, N. (2011) 'Suspect Communities'? Counter-Terrorism Policy, the Press and the Impact on Irish and Muslim Communities in Britain London: Metropolitan University, http://www.city.ac.uk/__data/assets/pdf_file/0005/96287/suspect-communities-report-july2011.pdf (accessed 2 April 2013).

Hillyard, P. (1993) *Suspect Community: People's Experience of the Prevention of Terrorism Acts in Britain*. London: Pluto Press.

—(2005) 'The "War on Terror:" Lessons from Ireland.' *Essays for Civil Liberties and Democracy in Europe, European Civil Liberties Network*, http://www.libertysecurity.org/IMG/pdf/The_War_on_Terror_lessons_from_Ireland.pdf (accessed 25 April 2010).

Home Office (2011) Prevent Strategy London: HMSO, https://www.gov.uk/government/uploads/system/uploads/attachment_data/file/97976/prevent-strategy-review.pdf (accessed 2 April 2013).

Innes, M., Abbot, L., Lowe, T. and Roberts, C. (2007) *Hearts and Minds and Eyes and Ears: Reducing Radicalisation Risks through Reassurance-Oriented Policing*. Cardiff: Cardiff University, Universities' Police Science Institute.

Innes, M., et al. (2011) *Assessing the Effects of Prevent Policing*. ACPO: Cardiff University, http://www.acpo.police.uk/documents/TAM/2011/PREVENT%20Innes%200311%20Final%20send%202.pdf (accessed 5 April 2013).

Jefferson, T., Walker, M. and Seneviratne, M. (1992) 'Ethnic Minorities, Crime and Criminal Justice: A Study in a Provincial City', in *Unravelling Criminal Justice*, edited by David Downes. London: Macmillan, pp. 138–64.

Jones, T. and Newburn, T. (2001) 'Widening Access: Improving Police Relations with Hard to Reach Groups' Paper 138, http://rds.homeoffice.gov.uk/rds/prgpdfs/prs138.pdf (accessed 25 April 2010).

Kundnani, A. (2009) *Spooked! How not to prevent violent extremism*. London: Institute of Race Relations.

Loader, I. (2006) 'Policing, Recognition and Belonging.' *The Annals of the American Academy of Political and Social Science* 605 (1): 201–21.

McDonald, L. Z. (2012) 'Engaging Young People within a Counter-Terrorism Context' in: B.Spalek (ed.) *Counter-Terrorism: community-based approaches to terror crime* Basingstoke: Palgrave MacMillan, pp. 90–136.

McGovern, M. (2010) Countering Terror or Counter-Productive? Comparing irish and British Muslim Experiences of Counter-Insurgency Law and Policy. Report of a Symposium held in Cultúrlann McAdam Ó Fiaich, Falls Road, Belfast, 23–24 June 2009. Lancashire: Edge Hill University.

Macpherson Inquiry (1999) *The Stephen Lawrence Inquiry, Report of an Inquiry by Sir William Macpherson of Cluny*, Cm 4262-I. London: Stationery Office, Parliamentary Papers.

Marshall, T. (1950) *Citizenship and Social Class* Milton Keynes: Open University Press.

Mythen, G. and Walklate, S. (2006) 'Criminology and Terrorism', *British Journal of Criminology* 46 (3): pp. 379–98.

Pantazis, C. and Pemberton, S. (2009) 'From the "Old" to the "New Suspect" Community: Examining the Impacts of Recent UK Counter-Terrorist Legislation' *British Journal of Criminology* 49 (5): 646–66.

Poynting, S. and Mason, V. (2008) 'The New Integrationism, the State and Islamophobia: Retreat from Multiculturalism in Australia', *International Journal of Law, Crime and Justice* 36 (4): 230–46.

Schmid, A. (2007) 'Terrorism and Democracy', *Terrorism and Political Violence* 10(3): 14–25.

Sharp, D. and Atherton, S. (2007) 'To Serve and Protect? The Experiences of Policing in the Community of Young People from Black and Other Ethnic Minority Groups.' *British Journal of Criminology* 47 (5): 746–63.

Sivanandan, A. (1981) 'From Resistance to Rebellion: Asian and Afro-Caribbean Struggles in Britain', *Race and Class* 23 (2–3): 111–52.

Smith, D. J. and Gray, J. (1985) *Police and People in London. The PSI Report*. Aldershot: Gower.

Spalek, B. (2008) *Communities, Identities and Crime* Bristol: Policy Press, pp. 1–241.

—(2010) 'Community Policing, Trust and Muslim Communities in relation to 'new terrorism' *Politics and Policy*, Vol. 38 (4), pp. 789–815.

Spalek, B., El-Awa, S. and McDonald, L. Z. (2009) *Engagement and Partnership Work in a Counter-Terrorism Context.* University of Birmingham.

Spalek, B. and Lambert, R. (2007) 'Muslim Communities under Surveillance: A stigmatised faith identity post 9/11' *Criminal Justice Matters: Security and Surveillance* No. 68, pp. 12–13.

Spalek, B. and McDonald, L. Z. (2011) 'Preventing Religio-Political Violent Extremism Amongst Muslim Youth: a study exploring police-community partnership' University of Birmingham.

Telegraph, The (2010) 'Police have apologized for putting 200 surveillance cameras in two largely Muslim neighbourhoods', 30 September 2010, http://www.telegraph.co.uk/news/uknews/law-and-order/8034999/Police-apologise-for-putting-200-CCTV-cameras-in-Muslim-area.html (accessed 11 May 2012).

Thacher, D. (2005) 'The Local Role in Homeland Security' 39 *Law & Society Review* (3): 635–75.

Thornton, S. (2010) *Project Champion Review*, 30 September 2010, http://www.west-midlands.police.uk/latest-news/docs/Champion_Review_FINAL_30_09_10.pdf (accessed 16 May 2012).

Virta, S. (2008) 'Community Policing Meets New Challenges', in *Policing Meets New Challenges: Preventing Radicalization and Recruitment*, edited by Sirpa Virta. Finland: University of Tampere, Department of Management Studies, CEPOL. 15–41.

Waddington, P. A. J., Stenson, K. and Don, D. (2004) 'In Proportion: Race, and Police Stop and Search' 44 (6): 889–914.

White House, The (2011) *National Strategy for CounterTerrorism*, http://www.whitehouse.gov/sites/default/files/counterterrorism_strategy.pdf (accessed 10 May 2012).

5

Police and Community Engagement and Partnerships for Counter-Terrorism

Introduction

Engagement and partnership are two key terms that feature significantly in the national counter-terrorism strategies of many countries, including EU member states, the US, Canada and Australia. Although these terms are often mentioned, with an implicit assumption that they are positive ways through which to achieve counter-terrorism strategies and goals, there is an absence of in-depth exploration of what engagement and partnership actually mean, and moreover, how those undertaking engagement and/or partnership are perceiving and experiencing these. This chapter aims to fill some of the gaps in knowledge regarding engagement and partnerships, particularly between community members and police officers who have been involved in counter-terrorism initiatives.

It is important to go beyond government rhetoric, to highlight the complexities and challenges of engagement and partnership work. As previously illustrated, the notion that 'communities can defeat terrorism' is prevalent within counter-terrorism policies and practices. Individuals, and the communities that they belong to, are being viewed as the moral agents of terrorism-prevention initiatives, responsible for building their own forms of resilience against violent extremism. How does this focus on communities, and the focus on responsible, active, citizens, as highlighted in the previous chapter, fit with engagement and partnership? Could it be that engagement and partnership, when applied to counter-terrorism and the focus on individual and community responsibility and resilience, is one-sided, in that it is communities that are expected to engage with state actors like the police, and to partner them, on terms that have already been set by government and/or state-led agendas? How much space is afforded to understandings of engagement and partnership that go beyond government rhetoric? Given that, increasingly, policing is viewed as a notion that involves not only policing agencies, but also other statutory agencies, and crucially, communities, what opportunities and challenges are there for engagement and partnerships? If security is something that is shared between police and other statutory agencies, and involves communities, it is therefore co-produced. What then are the purposes of engagement and partnerships? Might they be important mechanisms through which to enhance democratic policing that involves paying due regard to human rights issues, and the fostering of community well-being?

This chapter begins to explore some of these issues. First, a brief review of the wider literature on engagement and partnership in relation to policing is provided. This is followed by a discussion of engagement and partnership in relation to counter-terrorism, drawing upon the wider research literature as well as the presentation and discussion of data that has been collected from inter-views with police officers and community members. Whilst engagement and partnership can be carefully constructed with particular community members, it is key not to overlook the importance of police officers engaging generally with communities. Engagement and partnership can have several different interpretations and approaches, relating to enhancing the quality of life for communities, building inclusivity, developing connections with women, building relationships, engaging with wider political issues, moving at the community's pace, with respect and understanding. There can be tensions between 'hard-ended' intelligence-led approaches to counter-terrorism, in which community engagement and partnership are not priorities, and 'softer' community-focused approaches that are about relationship-building. Information sharing is a key issue for engagement and partnerships between police and communities.

Engagement and partnership in relation to policing

Unsurprisingly, there are many different understandings of what engagement and partnership mean and what they involve. For Wallerstein and Bernstein

(1988), community engagement suggests a process involving individuals, organisations and communities achieving power, not for domination but to act with others to implement change. The London-based thinktank, Demos, refers to police officers as needing to engage more substantially with political processes. This engagement is viewed as the ability of police officers 'to draw on work to which they are connected to shape explicit priorities on which they can focus and to allow other organisations and the public to help achieve them' (Edwards, 2006: 5). The work by Demos (Edwards, 2006) highlights the need for police officers not to view any engagement with politics as something negative, and equating this to political interference, but rather, to view political engagement as a means through which to share policing responsibilities.

Myhill (2004) offers the following definition of community engagement for policing policy:

> The process of enabling the participation of citizens and communities in policing at their chosen level, ranging from providing information and reassurance, to empowering them to identify and implement solutions to local problems and influence strategic priorities and decisions. The police, citizens, and communities must have the willingness, capacity and opportunity to participate. The Police Service and partner organisations must have a responsibility to engage and, unless there is a justifiable reason, the presumption is that they must respond to community input (Myhill, 2004: iv).

For Myhill (2004), there are three basic levels of community engagement: at the 'democratic mandate' level through which the involvement of community members is pursued; at the level of the neighbourhood, with a focus on local issues and priorities; and at the intermediate strategic level, which involves wider police service, regional and national issues and priorities. The wider context is important to consider, for this impacts substantially on policing. For example, in Britain, it was the previous Labour Government's focus on civil renewal that placed added emphasis on police and community engagement. In a speech on 11 June 2003, the former Home Secretary, David Blunkett, argued that communities should be empowered and active, with individuals increasingly determining the shape of their lives for themselves and the state taking on a supportive and facilitatory role. More recently, in 2011, the Conservative-Liberal Democrat Coalition Government introduced the notion of the Big Society, which is a vision for individuals and communities to have more power and responsibility to create better neighbourhoods and local services, in a radical shift of power away from the centre (Communities and Local Government, 2011). Whilst it is not the objective of this chapter to critique Big Society, the themes of responsibility and power shifting towards individuals and local communities seem to resonate with broader issues around engagement and partnership work in relation to policing. It may also be worth briefly mentioning Cook's (2006) analysis of community participation. According to Cook (2006: 124), community participation might be thought of as consisting of five levels: information (involves telling people what is planned), consultation (involves offering some options, listening to feedback, but not allowing new ideas), deciding together (providing opportunities for joint decision making), acting together (different interests form a partnership to carry out what they decide is best to do), and supporting independent community interests (local groups are offered funds, advice or other support to develop their own agendas within guidelines). For Cook, community participation often falls short, so that the fifth level, supporting independent community interests, is rarely put into practice. Importantly, managerial imperatives and strategic decisions on what can and cannot be done influence the scope of community participation. Moreover, market research-type consultation is often used, which for Cook (2006: 125) 'masks a patronising and complacent attitude to service users'. Furthermore, it is argued that communities, particularly Black and minority ethnic communities, might experience consultation overload, and at the same time might feel let down because the issues that they have raised during consultation have not been responded or listened to (Cook, 2006).

Edwards (2006) suggests that police need to improve on their partnership working as there is a diverse range of policing service providers, including the private sector, which can bring significant benefits. For Oppler (1997), partnership policing heralds a new development for policing which began in the 1980s, when the notion emerged of independent agents working together with formal structures that go beyond community policing models. The theme of localism features in Oppler's (1997) understanding of partnership policing, in that it is essential for partnership policing to be operationalised at a local level, which involves local actors adapting partnerships to fit their needs. For Oppler (1997), partnership policing, internationally, evolved out of a wider social and policy context which stressed that individuals are active citizens rather than welfare recipients, and so protection of life and property is the responsibility of citizens, aided by police. According to Oppler (1997: 13), partnership policing can be defined as 'a proactive leadership role in bringing disparate community groups such as the public, elected officials, government and other agencies together to focus on crime and community disorder problems'. Partnership policing is therefore about consultation, about involving citizens in the planning of policing, and about involving community leaders in deciding the policing priorities of local areas.

Thacher (2001) highlights some of the challenges facing police and community partnerships. A key issue for partnership is that it can involve a wide variety of partners who have their own institutional, cultural, political and other values, and so there is the potential for conflict between partners as a result of competing values. It is not just a question of competing values but also of competing priorities, with different partners often having different sets of priorities. Thacher (2001) argues that some researchers suggest that partnerships within a policing context are not possible because values and goals can be so incompatible. For Thacher (2001), exploring how tensions are resolved and how competing values can be legitimately managed is a key area for research, policy and practice. For instance, it may be that police agencies can shift their priorities in order to make them more acceptable to communities (which may involve a movement away from 'crime-fighting' towards embracing a more holistic policing approach focusing on safety); it may also involve pursuing competing aims and thus working within a more pluralistic environment (Thacher, 1998). Partnership can also involve partner agencies making their resources available to each other, thereby enabling all partners to benefit. A key challenge to confront is that of where the balance should lie between liberty and order, with policing aims being defined broadly enough to encompass both (Thacher, 1998). It is also important to note that if we understand partnership to mean equality, transparency and legitimate cooperation between partners, then achieving this may be challenging because of power differentials: in the case of police-focussed work, community groups may not feel that they are actual partners in the process. In cases where there are power imbalances between partners it is important for those in positions of relative power to create spaces within which all partners are equals and included

(Spalek, El-Alwa and McDonald 2009). This is especially important in the context of police-community engagement as police officers are in positions of relative power over community members. The extent to which police and community engagement and partnerships involve supporting independent community interests, particularly within a counter-terrorism context, is an interesting question, and one which raises another: given that the notion of community itself is complex and contested, whose independent interests are being supported? As illustrated in chapter 2, for counter-terrorism work to be effective it is important to include credible partners, and the independent interests of these partners might comprise radical approaches and solutions that national governments may find problematic. If police officers are to engage increasingly with politics, therefore, they run the risk of being criticised for supporting radical groups and interests, which may alienate wider communities from the police (Thacher, 2001).

Engagement and partnership in relation to counter-terrorism

The national counter-terrorism policies of many countries, including the UK, US, Canada and Australia, refer to the notions of engagement and partnership. Localism, the importance of connecting governments and communities, and connecting diverse state and non-state actors, are all themes that feature in national counter-terrorism strategies in relation to the notions of engagement and partnership. For instance, in the Australian Counter-Terrorism White Paper (2010) it is argued that 'the Government recognises that strong partnerships between all levels of government and communities are critical to success, and that solutions must be appropriate to local circumstances'. In CONTEST, the UK's main national counter-terrorism strategy, engagement and partnership is referred to on many occasions. For instance, on page 1 the document claims that 'the Government is therefore working in partnership with Muslim communities to help them prevent extremists gaining influence there'. CONTEST also refers to partnerships between police and other state agencies and also with the charitable and voluntary sectors, thus 'developing and delivering this counter-terrorism strategy involves all parts of

Government acting together and taking a joined-up approach to dealing with this complex and wide-ranging threat. Delivery also depends upon partnerships with the police and emergency services, local authorities, and devolved administrations, as well as with the private sector and the voluntary and charitable sector' (HM Government, 2006: 5). In the Prevent Review 2011, engagement and partnership is regularly referred to. An interesting aspect of the Prevent Review 2011 is that a distinction is made between criteria for funding and criteria for engagement:

> We would emphasise that criteria for funding are different from criteria for engagement (such as contact and dialogue). There may be cases where the Government judge that there is a need to engage with groups or individuals whom it would never choose to fund. That may particularly be the case overseas, where we may need to engage with groups or individuals that are seen as moderate in their own country but not in the UK. (HM Government, 2011: 40)

Of course, what is meant by 'moderate' and what is meant by 'extreme' is unclear, and is likely to be politically dictated (Spalek and McDonald, 2010). The theme of localism in relation to partnership can be found in the Prevent Review thus:

> We expect all local areas to have a partnership tasked to take forward work on Prevent using the most appropriate structure in their area and to a level which is proportionate to local risk. Wherever possible, the partnership should comprise social services, policing, children's services, youth services, UKBA, representatives from further and higher education, probation services, schools, local prisons, health and others as required by local need (HM Government, 2011: 100).

Multi-agency work is therefore a key aspect to counter-terrorism policy and practice in the UK. This is particularly evidenced by the Channel Project, which is a controversial national scheme established to support those individuals vulnerable to recruitment by violent extremists, using the resources and experience of professionals who provide an ongoing support package. Described as a multi-agency process with a diverse grouping involving police, social services, health, youth offending team workers and community individuals, the group is mostly chaired by a local authority employee or a community person with sensitive case details provided by the police. Whilst some Channel panels have community involvement, the police remain nervouse about issues around security clearance, data protection (around legislative impact), confidentiality and extent of Criminal Records Bureau (CRB) checks, due to the sensitive nature of casework data on vulnerable individuals being shared in a non-police domain, even if they are counter-terrorism partners (Kundnani, 2009). In the US counter-terrorism strategy, engagement and partnership is also discussed, in relation not only to state and non-state local partners in the US, but also in relation to state and non-state global partners, thus:

> We will work closely with local and global partners, inside and outside govern-ments, to discredit al-Qa'ida ideology and reduce its resonance. We will put forward a positive vision of engagement with foreign publics and support for universal rights that demonstrates that the United States aims to build while al-Qa'ida would only destroy (The White House, 2011: 10).

Locally, US policy includes engaging and partnering with communities as there is the belief that this can help protect communities from being influ-enced by AQ and its affiliates:

> We are working to bring to bear many of these capabilities to build reslilience withing our communitites here at home against al-Qa'ida-inspired radicali-zation, recruitment, and mobilization to violence. Although increasing our engagement and partnership with communities can help protect them from the influence of al-Qa'ida and its affiliates and adherents, we must ensure that we remain engaged in the full range of community concerns and interests. (The White House, 2011: 11)

As highlighted in the previous chapter, however, police counter-terrorism efforts in the US have been criticised for infiltrating American Muslims and for placing them under surveillance without any valid investigative justifi-cation. It is therefore difficult to link the US policy discourse with the lived realities of many American Muslims.

Globally, Pakistan and Afghanistan are, in particular, mentioned in relation to partnership work:

> We will defeat al-Qa'ida only through a sustained partnership with Pakistan. The underlying conditions that allow the group to maintain its safe haven and regenerate—including its ability to capitalize on relationships with militant allies—can only be addressed through a sustained local presence opposed to

al-Qaʻida. Pakistan has shown resolve in this fight in the face of increasing brutality by al-Qaʻida and its Pakistan-based allies, but greater Pakistani–U.S. strategic cooperation across a broader range of political, military, and economic pursuits will be necessary to achieve the defeat of al-Qaʻida in Pakistan and Afghanistan. (The White House, 2011, 13)

Again, this rhetoric fails to reflect the reality, with the relationship between Pakistan and the US being one far from the ideal of partnership. Any relationship-building between the US and Pakistan has come under severe strain as a result of a number of crises linked to counter-terrorism including the killing of Osama Bin Laden and the US use of unmanned drones.

Engagement and partnership within a counter-terrorism context raise a number of issues and questions. As demonstrated in chapter 2, engagement and partnership can be carefully constructed and extremely sensitive, rather than comprised of a wide-sweeping engagement and partnership approach that the notion ʻcommunities can defeat terrorism' might imply. Engagement and partnership can be aimed in particular at credible community members, who have reach into spaces and groups that are perhaps impenetrable to the police and other state actors. State actors may rely heavily on engagement and partnerships with credible community members, as a way of trying to implement community-based counter-terrorism initiatives. The following quotation taken from an interview with a police officer, in which he referes to a mentoring scheme targeted at individuals deemed at significant risk of violent radicalisation, further demonstrates the importance of credibility:

> I used the old golf club analogy ... you've got ... a young Afghan male who's stuck in the rough and you think, crikey I need someone, I need a mentor who understands totally where he's coming from, because that person themselves may have come from Afghanistan, they're an illegal immigrant, has settled, knows all the pitfalls, knows all the issues, knows what comes from that same area of Afghanistan, so can empathise, so it's like who have we got in our golf club? Oh yeah, the six iron, ... the Afghan, yeah. And then they sort of put them in touch. So, very simply said, but you know, we're trying to find all these different people now we can call upon in situations to come and help.

Perhaps this is why the UK Prevent Review 2011 highlights that there is a distinction between criteria for funding and criteria for engagement. Implicit in this approach is an understanding that government needs to engage with credible community members who, for a wide range of reasons, may be deemed by the British Government not to warrant funding. This links to a point made in a Demos report on community-based approaches to counter-terrorism, in which the authors argue that there is a need to move away from an all-encompassing notion of 'the community' and towards engaging more openly with faith-based groups, including those on the periphery such as Salafis (Briggs et al., 2006).

Whilst this discussion highlights the importance of developing engagement with credible community members, it is imperative not to lose sight of the importance of general engagement with communities. The information that is elicited here by police may lack specificity, but may provide them with general background information about what is happening within communities. This is illustrated by the following quotation from an interview with an overt counter-terrorism police officer:

> I pick up – I was saying to one of our analysts, every day when I go and speak to somebody in the community I learn something from them. Feedback to yourself. You absorb that information.

Engagement can also be about enhancing the quality of life of community members, as the following quotation from an interview with a counter-terrorism police officer illustrates:

> a local intelligence team which is a team which develops an intimate under-standing of who our communities are, where they are, and to the best of our ability what the current issues are affecting them. Where they congregate, how we best engage with them, how we communicate effectively, just all of those dynamics, you know, just to ensure that we're not just relying on ten year old census data, but we're actually monitoring to say who are communities, where are they coming from, what are the tensions, how are we impacting on tensions and what can we do to play a part in enhancing everybody's quality of life?

The following quotation is from a community member in relation to the Muslim safety Forum, a forum through which community members in London engaged regularly with senior police officers of the Metropolitan Police Service. This quotation illustrates how engagement can be about inclu-sivity, involving a wide variety of individuals from within communities:

> even within the organisation, some are huge organisations that are part of MSF,

some are very small. But everybody brings a different flavour. Everybody brings their different concerns. Some are very vocal. You have the angry young men, you have the mild women there and you have the angry women there. You have lots of different personalities there. Some people come to observe because they come purely to learn.

However, this same community member also demonstrates the difficulties in engaging Muslim women:

And some people say we purely come to see what is going on because even the I'm not someone who's very vocal, I don't like crowds, I can't … it's usually the women that say I can't really engage in that sense, I don't want to be heard. Not because I'm a Muslim woman and we can't talk, and things like that. It's not that, it's because I don't feel comfortable and not everyone is gifted with that kind of you know becoming the speaker or becoming that person that can lead the herd, so to speak. Not everybody has that kind of ability or is comfortable with that kind of attention. And so they say we'll come to learn and we take it back and then within our own organisations that we can do something. And it's also good to know what's going on around us for that. But I think I do see through MSF the Muslim organisations very much are a boy's club and I do wonder sometimes why? Is it because the women are so reluctant to come forward because the brothers will always say no, we want more women, but do you really?

The following quotation comes from an interview with a Muslim woman who is part of a women's organisation that is a member of the Muslim Safety Forum. This quotation highlights how the priorities of the organisation that she was representing on the Muslim Safety Forum were different from those of the police:

So in terms of representing X and the partnership work with the police, our focus was slightly different in that we represented a certain part of the community whose needs were different from the needs of the police in terms of what angle they wanted to work with the community and especially with women. Ours was social need, emotional and physical to some extent, whereas obviously for the police their primary concern is safety and security.

Despite having different priorities, this same community member argues that partnership was possible with the police. Basically, the police could work with this particular Muslim women's organisation to help women in relation to domestic violence issues while the organisation could provide the police with access to women:

So in some ways we did link up whereas we were dealing with people who had, women who had domestic violence issues and things so we found a common ground from which we could develop partnership work. What they wanted to do was have access to, all the women could come to us … through X we have access to a lot of women and young women who are professionals as well as young mothers, mainly English speaking women, but we have access to the older generation as well who the police would never be able to access because of the language barrier or because these women do not come out. So we formed to some extent a partnership where we could give them that access and they can give us the support in terms of developing certain projects that we felt that they can help us with. And mainly obviously with certain areas like domestic violence where they can really give us some key information and support. So this is just from my individual partnership work that was developed with the police as a result of developing the Muslim Safety Forum.

Police officers' and community members' understandings of partnership and engagement is an area that has been examined in the body of research underpinning this book. There is a focus on 'trust-building, equality and mutual benefit' in partnerships, 'space, recognition and acceptance of diverse political and religious beliefs and identities' as well as 'emotion, political and social grievance, religion and spirituality and personal perspectives' (Spalek, El-Alwa and McDonald, 2009: 84–5). The following quotation from a community member illustrates that it takes time to build relationships, and that real engagement is what matters:

> I think one of the things is due to an enormous amount of openness and I think it's about a time piece. You build a relationship over time, you don't just turn up, you know, you turn up at the mosque once, no, you go every Friday and you're there every Friday, you come as friendly, you go on the open days. That's kinda … it's that real engagement bit.

For the following police officer, engagement is about sitting down and chatting with people:

> this is just good coppering again really, sitting down and having a cup of tea with people and you know, you're putting the world to rights aren't you?

For this same police officer engagement is also about discussing wider political issues:

> And I agree, I mean I sit down with people and I think our foreign policy is

bloody rubbish, and that a lot of it has added to all the woes of what we've got now ... until we actually really say, well yeah we went to Iraq and okay Iraq wasn't a perfect place to start with and he was a murdering bastard, but what on earth – we've just opened up a hornet's nest now that will never go away, and has really upset hundreds of thousands of people all round the world, even though we went in ostensibly for doing the right thing, very ill conceived, not thought through, and now, you know, the country's just in total turmoil, and those wounds will probably never heal.

The officer also argues that engagement with Muslim communities should be no different than engagement with other faith communities:

... if the copper at the mosque having a cup of tea you know, he's saying the same thing, but it's no – it is no different really, it shouldn't be any different, and I think this is probably one of the positives as well ... you're at the local church having a cup of tea with the vicar and you're talking about the graffiti on the grave stones, and you know, and trying to sort that problem out, it shouldn't be really any different than having a cup of tea at the mosque and we're talking about other aspects of criminality which terrorism and the violent extremism is.

One community member refers to partnership involving a common understanding of people working together, of statutory agencies not 'going off and doing things':

... there is a common and shared understanding of the relationships of people working together. And where there isn't a hierarchy of, say, it's a partnership but the statutory organisations are the dominant partners or that they will just tap into the community as and when they see fit ... which is something that happens quite a lot. And also it's a partnership that's got to be consistent because you will have, in my own experience, you'll have some kind of very productive moments and you'll have other moments where the statutory organisations will just go off and do things, or they'll take certain decisions.

This person goes on to highlight how in many instances statutory agencies can undertake activities on their own, with community members having to try and keep tabs on what is happening, reminding agencies that they are supposed to be in partnership:

And, more often than not, the community partners are always chasing them up or kind of saying, 'Well, have you forgotten we're in a partnership? And how could you justify that action, or those set of actions, or those behaviours when we're meant to be in a partnership together?'

The following community member emphasises the need to move at the community's pace:

> I think in the early days it may have felt as if the police and the local authority wanted to dominate things, to do things their way and we've constantly said no, you can't move quickly, you have to wait until the community are ready to move on these sort of issues, to accept the potential benefits, but in their own time and not to feel that you can impose yourself on people until they're ready to identify there may be some value.

This same community member also speaks about the importance of there being 'trustworthy engagement', that any powers that the police and local authorities have should be used wisely:

> But those values emerge through the process of engagement, trustworthy engagement with the communities and the communities feel reassured by this sense that there are powers but those powers are going to be used with a kind of wisdom and understanding rather than without sufficient thought and certain care really.

Another community member speaks about the importance of respect and understanding for partnership:

> I think a lot of that depends on a sense of fairness and integrity on all sides really. And I think you only really feel we're reaching these things when people are treating each other with that high level of respect and understanding.

The following police officer highlights the challenges facing police in trying to go beyond talking to people who want to engage with police but who may not be connected at a wider grassroots level:

> the disadvantage for police consultation in my book, and I speak with some experience here, is we talk to the people who will talk to us … unfortunately there are people out there with single-issue agendas. There are people out there who are not actually what they purport to be. They say they're plugged into the community. They say they can represent a particular community. They actually represent nobody but themselves and maybe one or two others. There are people who have information that is at least 20 years out of date and they're still fighting the battles of 1981 as opposed to dealing with the issues of 2010.

This same police officer also highlights that often engagement is with the same people, even though they may not be the most suitable:

> And I've encountered all of these while I've, you know ... and, and another problem is that you actually end up engaging with the same people with different hats on. So that's why you need to go out into the community, identify the people and get them on board and get them talking to the consultative groups and represented there so that they can actually have their views represented.

The following police officer speaks about how community engagement has not traditionally been viewed by police as worthy of significant attention, for police like to see themselves as crime-fighting agents:

> Empathy and understanding ... it's police officers, without using the word not politically, but are conservative, traditional, shall we say, very much ... and you have to sell it sometimes ... you know, the soft skills are not popular with them; they're seen as becoming soft on things.

This same police officer argues, however, that community engagement should not be viewed as a soft option but, rather, as just as important as arresting people because hard policing powers need to be carried out within a wider understanding of how such powers impact upon communities:

> Well actually it's not. It's about doing your job. It's about getting out there and arresting the bad guys. But it's about not upsetting everybody else in the process. It's about avoiding collateral damage. It's about sensitivity about why people might feel bad about 3 o'clock in the morning, 14 people dressed like the storm troopers out of Star Wars beating down someone's door and dragging them off, you know, the next door neighbour, dragging them off with all the noise and everything else and disruption that that entails ... there's still work to be done with the police around that but there again, I think probably we do better than we're given credit for in that way.

The following quotation from an interview with a counter-terrorism police officer further highlights the importance of considering the wider impact of counter-terrorism laws and operations on communities:

> I mean that was one of the things after 2001 where we had draconian powers that were introduced, or fairly sort of relatively draconian powers ... a lot of people were arrested without charge, you were very quickly noticing in the community that more time was spent worrying about the impact of these

operations on the community because that's what impact them on a day to day event, than actually trying to solve the problem of preventing people putting bombs down on buses.

The officer goes on to talk about the importance of considering the impact that counter-terrorism operations have on communities, because terrorists wish to use any local grievances about counter-terrorism strategies as a recruitment tool:

> you're fighting the terrorist wish to recruit from minorities, so you are trying to counter them getting recruits from the community ... the community need to be onside because ... I mean terrorism is propaganda of the deed, the deed, in a way, is ... a small part of the issue is the fear, the wider ramifications of terrorism that ... that you're trying to counter and one of the things is that the terrorists want people to be frightened so that they change their mind. So they want people in communities to feel threatened by ... anti terrorism, you know, the impact of anti terrorism.

The officer also talks about how building relationships with community members can help police to separate out what is a real terrorist threat from what is a community issue:

> I think the third thing is that communities are a source of information and I think that's one of the things where Prevent is ... we've slightly missed the ... missed the point that you can't police, you can't make good decisions without having good information. And the community provide information, and they also enable you to prove negatives because there aren't millions of terrorists out there but we have to have the best possible information and intelligence in order to focus on the people that matter. And if you have good information and good relationships with communities, you can get rid of, you know, hopefully, and this is the theory, that you cannot spend a lot of time wasted on pursuing negative leads 'cause people will say well that's a ... dispute, it's not a terrorist issue, they're just bubbling the other people up because they don't like them.

Tensions between 'hard-ended' intelligence-led approaches to counter-terrorism, in which community engagement and partnership are not priorities, and 'softer' community-focussed approaches that are about relationship-building, have been highlighted by Dame Eliza Manningham-Butler, a former Director General of MI5 who argued that:

For the Police Service, community engagement is quite properly an important part of the response to this wider challenge. But inevitably of course, there will be times when intelligence-based activity targeted at a specific element within the community, a tiny minority, of course, will rub up uncomfortably against initiatives to engage with the community more broadly. This is likely to be a recurring theme in counter-terrorist work in the UK in the years ahead (Manningham-Butler, 2007: 45 in Vertigans, 2010: 31).

It is perhaps worth distinguishing between proactive and reactive styles of engagement, as identified in a study examining police and community partnerships within a counter-terrorism context (Spalek, El-Alwa and McDonald 2009). Proactive engagement is 'where communities become actively involved in the development of particular initiatives with police, having a decision-making role whereby communities are consulted and actively engaged at all stages of a project, from initial conceptualisation through to development and implementation' (Spalek, El-Alwa and McDonald, 2009: 27). A further example of proactive engagement is in relation to communities moderating police approaches. The following quotation is taken from an interview with an overt counter-terrorism police officer, who explains the importance of proactively engaging:

Everybody brings their expertise, their disposition, to the table. That's very healthy, you know, for cops to be sitting there and understanding what else is out there so that they can help to moderate their approaches as well.

The importance of proactive engagement is further highlighted in the following quotation from an overt counter-terrorism police officer, who argues that families, friends, communities are the long-term solution to terrorism:

Because terrorism, we can work all day, especially the police, and you can have engagement, you can have good community links. But when it comes to information or people actually preventing it, it has to be that family link; it has to be those parents; it has to be the community; it has to be the friends. It has to be that ground level to prevent it long term.

Reactive engagement is where 'communities respond to initiatives that have already been developed and events that have already taken place, so that feedback is sought by police from communities rather than active involvement in decision-making – providing information to communities and consulting them for their feedback rather than police and communities deciding and acting together' (Spalek, El-Alwa and McDonald, 2009: 27–8). Whereas some community members and police officers can prefer a proactive style of engagement, others can prefer a reactive style of engagement. This means that at the same time that some community members and police officers will be actively pursuing and adopting a proactive style of engagement, other community members and police officers will be actively pursuing and adopting a reactive style of engagement. This can therefore lead to some confusion and even frustration between individuals. It is therefore important to set out the style and terms of engagement at the outset, or to at least have a discussion about this. It is also likely that the aims of engagement differ. It may be that some community members and police officers view engagement as a forum through which to air grievances, it may be that some see engagement as exploring cases of potential police abuses of power, whilst for others engagement may be seen as a means through which to build relationships (Spalek, El-Alwa and McDonald, 2009). The goal of collaboration is to promote 'open channels of honest, long-term communication and the ability to negotiate conflict and different goals or values' but 'without compromising the fundamental standpoint of partners' (Spalek, El-Alwa and McDonald, p. 85). Moreover, it is very important that officers have good interpersonal skills when cooperating with community members (Silk, 2009).

Those community members and organisations involved in engagement with police officers may need support for capacity-building in order to enable them to communicate more effectively with the police and other statutory agencies. This point links to the notion of empowerment, which Pinderhughes (1995: 136) understands as referring to 'achieving reasonable control over one's destiny, learning to cope constructively with debilitating forces in society, and acquiring the competence to initiate change at the individual and systems levels'. Spalek, El-Alwa and McDonald (2009) highlight the importance of empowerment within a counter-terrorism context, providing examples of police officers playing a key role in empowering community members to tackle threats from terrorism. One example of this might be when community members discuss their ideas for community projects with police officers around how to prevent violent extremism, with police officers providing vital feedback and then support as to how to go about developing projects further and gaining funding for them. This kind of activity might be viewed as a form of capacity building within communities, facilitated by police and other partners. Spalek, El-Alwa and McDonald's study (2009) found that, as a secondary benefit, this form of community empowerment can directly lead to intelligence for the police. It is important to stress the primacy of community empowerment over community intelligence in order to build effective partnerships based on trust between police and communities. Any mistrust that might be generated through a desire to focus on gathering information will directly impact on police officers' abilities to pick up on voluntary, and thus more reliable, community intelligence in the long term (Spalek, El-Alwa and McDonald, 2009).

Engagement and partnership between police officers and community members within a counter-terrorism context also raises the question of information sharing. The counter-terrorism arena is one that is dominated by secrecy, and yet with the introduction of overt styles of countering terrorism, police officers are engaging and partnering community members. It is important to stress that overtness is appreciated whilst covertness can create barriers between police and community (Silk, 2009). Silk (2009) has argued that it is important to be upfront about the police assignments in the community. Silk (2009) also shows that officers claim that the success of overt strategies lie in officers' abilities to explain the nature of the assignment in a comprehensible manner. Innes et al. (2011) also have noted that police officers experience positive public responses to more open ways of working, reflecting how officers involved in more covert strategies have to negotiate complex 'back-stage' and 'front-stage' arrangements. Information sharing between police and communities is a key dilemma, and police officers and community members can grapple with what information to provide to each other, and what the wider implications of this may be. Safeguards need to be placed around information-sharing. For example, community members who engage and even partner with police and who provide information can be placing themselves at considerable risk of reprisals from members of their own communities or any networks that they belong to, with the potential of them being labelled as spies or informants. Police officers are also potentially placing themselves at risk from community-instigated and other reprisals (Spalek and McDonald, 2011). It may be that within a counter-terrorism arena all engagement and partnership places individuals at risk, hence there need to be in place procedures that can help mitigate some of the risks posed by information sharing (see Baker, 2011; 2012 for further analysis).

A further issue in counter-terrorism is whether the question of values should influence whether or not, and to what extent, engagement and partnership should take place. For Briggs et al. (2006), whilst values may be difficult to align, 'we must not let them get in the way of the priority of tackling terrorism. The energy of these non-violent forms of mobilisation must be harnessed towards this shared goal.' Similarly, Spalek and Lambert (2008) have argued that broader questions about community and social cohesion, alongside discussions about national identity, should not define the terms of engagement with Muslim communities for the purposes of counter-terrorism. Instead, a rational assessment should be made according to which groups can best help combat extremism, and questions of cohesion and national identity should be left to other fields of policy-making. However, the Muslim Contact Unit, an overt counter-terrorism policing unit that engaged and partnered with Salafi and Islamist Muslim groups, attracted considerable media and policy attention and criticism, being labeled as 'appeasers of extremism' (Lambert, 2008: 6). According to Silvestri (2007), Salafism in particular has been used as a synonym for jihadism and terrorism, and yet there are important nuances and many different positionings of Salafis, alongside the evolution of different currents of Islamic thought. It might be argued that to draw upon and use Islamic identities and practices that potentially might be construed as 'radical' (in some cases simply because individuals are religiously conservative and have a real or a perceived opposition to established secular values (see Spalek, Lambert, and Baker 2009)) runs the risk that these are negatively labelled and might be considered to require counter-insurgency and/or countersubversion tactics (Spalek, 2011). For Kilcullen (2007: 112–13), counter-insurgency involves 'all measures adopted to suppress an insurgency' where insurgency is 'a struggle to control a contested political space, between a state (or group of states or occupying powers) and one or more popularly based, non-state challengers'. For Lambert (2008) a counter-subversion perspective in the UK posits that those described as being Islamist, whether or not they are suspected of terrorism or violent extremism, are to be targeted and stigmatised in the same way as terrorists influenced or directed by AQ. Clearly, these debates can significantly influence police and community engagement and partnership. Spalek, El-Alwa and McDonald (2009) have argued that:

> If experienced counter-terrorism practitioners see a benefit in engaging with Muslim minorities at the margins of communities, reasoning that the foundational goal of preventing violence is shared, and such groups and individuals are in a position to assist and contribute to the prevention of violence and related activities, other agendas become entirely peripheral. In particular, the concern that a group may follow a theological methodology, or share a political sympathy or aim related in some way to those perpetrating and supporting violence does not negate the necessity of engagement. Even in light of confident democratic principles which allow for marginal voices within the boundaries of law and order, the fundamental point is whether or not terrorist violence is condoned or condemned (Malik 2008) (In Spalek, El-Alwa and McDonald, 2009: 62).

Moreover, it may be that engaging marginal and marginalised Muslim groups such as Salafis and Islamists is a logical approach within a community-focussed response to countering terrorism, involving faith-based approaches to youth work, education and de-radicalisation central to the Prevent agenda (Spalek, El-Alwa and McDonald, 2009). The following quotation is taken from an interview with a counter-terrorism police officer who stresses the risks involved in engaging with some 'radicals' who may have negative views of homosexuality for example:

> whilst we might actually want to support someone that perhaps we wouldn't possibly endorse all their views because I mean again you may have a mainstream Wahabist cleric who has credibility within the community who totally rejects Al Qaeda extremist philosophy but has what we would consider as rather unenlightened views about homosexuals, women or whatever. And we would need to engage and seek their support to put the message out. But it does need to be managed quite carefully because of the risk of embarrassment and also the risk of wrecking any influence that they have. We want to try and keep the influence going if it's a positive influence. We try to downplay the negative.

The following is a quotation taken from another interview with a counter-terrorism police officer, who makes a distinction between the viewpoints of the pragmatists and the theorists in terms of this issue of 'engaging with radicals':

> sometimes I think the divide is between the theorists and the pragmatists. The pragmatists are the people ... where they know where they're going on a day

to day basis. The theorists are people who worry where are we actually gonna end up? And I think theorists ... have a danger of being exactly the same as Islamists and anybody who ... has an idea of progress, that we are aiming to have a society in the future and you're not actually gonna be part of it, I think is, you know, you've gotta be very careful how you articulate your end goal because ... that's what ideologies are about. But on the other hand you do have to think, well, about engaging with this group and not that group, are we actually making the problem worse than better? I mean my aim is to have a London that is ... diverse, safe and all those things but how you actually articulate, measure that ... how do you know that what you're doing today is actually achieving a safe and diverse capital city?

The above quotation demonstrates the challenges involved in any kind of preventative work, for it is difficult to be able to prove that any work being undertaken today will have an impact in terms of building a safer society in the future. Senior counter-terrorism police officers have to take certain risks themselves, implementing novel prevention initiatives that need to be tested out without any guarantees of effectiveness or success.

Conclusion

This chapter has focussed on engagement and partnership within a counter-terrorism context, these being two key themes that feature significantly in the national counter-terrorism strategies of many different countries. It has examined engagement and partnership in more detail, drawing on the wider research literature as well as presenting empirical data gathered from interviews with counter-terrorism police officers and community members. Key themes highlighted in this chapter in relation to engagement and partnership include: the importance of general engagement with wide-ranging community members; the importance and challenges of engaging and partnering non-violent radicals; how engagement and partnership can have several different meanings and approaches relating to enhancing the quality of life for communities, building inclusivity, developing connections with women, building relationships, engaging with wider political issues, moving at the community's pace, with respect and understanding. There can be tensions between 'hard-ended' intelligence-led approaches to counter-terrorism, in which community engagement and partnership are not priorities, and 'softer' community-focused approaches that are about relationship-building. Information sharing is a key issue for engagement and partnerships. Clearly, these issues relate to questions around the implementation of democratic forms of policing which respect human rights and which seek to foster community well-being. This chapter demonstrates the centrality of security as something that is co-produced. It is therefore perhaps more helpful to view counter-terrorism as conflict transformation, for engagement and partnership illustrates how the prevention of terrorism is about understanding community dynamics, about helping communities to deal with wide-ranging issues, and about facilitating dialogue and relationship-building between police officers and community members. The next chapter explores police and community engagement further in relation to understanding emotions.

Bibliography

Australian Counter-Terrorism Strategy (2010) http://www.dpmc.gov.au/publications/counter_terrorism/3_strategy.cfm (accessed 10 April 2013).

Briggs, R., Fieschi, C. and Lownsbrough, H. (2006) *Bringing it Home Community-Based Approaches to Counter-Terrorism*. London: DEMOS.

Communities and Local Government (2011) 'Building the Big Society', http://www.communities.gov.uk/communities/bigsociety/ (accessed 22 June 2012).

Cook, D. (2006) Criminal and Social Justice, London: Sage.

Edwards, C. (2006) 'The Activist Police Force', in J. Craig (ed.) *The Everyday Encounters of Citizens and Professionals Should Help Them to Build Autonomy.* London: Demos, pp. 52–60.

HM Government (2006) *Countering International Terrorism: The United Kingdom's Strategy*, July (presented to Parliament by the Prime Minister and the Secretary of State for the Home Department by Command of Her Majesty).

—(2011) *Prevent Strategy Review*, London: Her Majesty's Stationery Office CM8092.

Innes, M., Innes, T. and Roberts, C. with T. Lowe and S. Lakhani (2011) *Assessing the Effects of Prevent Policing: A Report to the Association of Chief Police Officers.* Universities' Police Science Institute Cardiff: Cardiff University.

Kilcullen, D. (2007) 'Counter-insurgency', *Survival*, 48, 4, pp. 111–30.

Kundnani, A. (2009) *Spooked! How not to prevent violent extremism*, London: Institute of Race Relations.

Lambert, R. (2008) 'Empowering Salafis and Islamists against Al-Qaida: A London Counter-Terrorism Case Study', *PS: Political Science and Politics* 41(1): 31–5.

Myhill, A. (2004) Community Engagement in Policing: Lessons from the Literature. London: Home Office.

Oppler, S. (1997) 'Partners Against Crimr: From Community to Partnership Policing'. Crime and Policing Project, Institute for Security Studies, Occasional Paper No. 16 (March), http://dspace.cigilibrary.org/jspui/bitstream/123456789/31596/1/paper_16.pdf?1 (accessed 6 January 2012).

Pinderhughes, E. B. (1983) 'Empowerment for our Clients and for Ourselves: Social Casework', Journal of Contemporary Social Work, 64(6): 331–8.

Silk, D. (2009) 'Outreach between Muslim Communities and Police in the UK: Preliminary Report', https://getd.libs.uga.edu/pdfs/silk_phillip_d_201005_phd/silk_phillip_d_201005_phd.pdf (accessed 3 April 2013).

Silvestri, S. (2007) 'Radical Islam: threats and opportunities', *Global Dialogue*, 9, 3–4, pp. 118–26.

Spalek, B. (2011) 'New Terrorism' and Crime Prevention Initiatives Involving Muslim Young People in the UK: Research and Policy Contexts, *Religion, State and Society*, 39(2–3), pp. 191–207.

Spalek, B., El-Awa, S. and McDonald, L. Z. (2009) 'Engagement and Partnership Work in a Counter-Terrorism Context'. Birmingham: University of Birmingham.

Spalek, B. and Lambert, B. (2008) 'Muslim Communities, Counter-terrorism and De-radicalisation: A Reflective Approach to Engagement' *International Journal of Law, Crime and Justice* Vol. 36 (4) pp. 257–70.

Spalek, B. and McDonald, L. Z. (2010) 'Anti-Social Behaviour Powers and the Policing of Security'. *Social Policy and Society* 9 (1): 123–33.

—(2011) 'Preventing Religio-Political Violent Extremism Amongst Muslim Youth: a study exploring police-community partnership'. Birmingham: University of Birmingham.

Spalek, B., Lambert, R. and Baker, A. H. (2009) 'Minority Muslim Communities and Criminal Justice: Stigmatized UK Faith Identities Post 9/11 and 7/7', in H. S. Bhui (ed.), *Race and Criminal Justice*. London: Sage, pp. 170–87.

Thacher, D. (1998) 'Developing Community Partnerships: Value Conflicts in 11 Cities'. Program in Criminal Justice Policy and Management of the Malcolm Wiener Center for Social Policy: John F. Kennedy School of Government, Harvard University. Working Paper #98-05-15.

—(2001) 'Conflicting Values in Community Policing', *Law and Society Review*, 35(4): 765–98.

Vertigans, S. (2010) 'British Muslims and the UK Government's "War on Terror" Within: Evidence of a Clash of Civilizations or Emergent De-civilizing Processes.' *The British Journal of Sociology*, 61 (1): 24–44.

Wallerstein, N. and Bernstein, E. (1988) Empowerment education: Freire's idea adapted to health education. *Health Education Quarterly*, 15(4), 379–94.

White House, The (2011) *National Strategy for Counter-Terrorism*, http://www. whitehouse.gov/sites/default/files/counterterrorism_strategy.pdf (accessed 10 May 2012).

6

Understanding Emotions in Counter-Terrorism Practice

Introduction

The role of emotions in relation to terrorism has generated some research and policy interest. Emotions have been discussed in connection with he tactics used by terrorists to generate wider fear within a society, to spread panic and destabilise states (Hülsse and Spencer, 2008). There has also been some research attention given to the role of emotions in political agency and the ways in which emotions may have played a part in the violent radicalisation of terrorists (Wright-Neville-and Smith, 2009). The emotions generated in the researcher when undertaking research on terrorism have also been discussed (Silke, 2001; Toros, 2008). Additionally, grievances within communities have also been given some attention, particularly in relation to their role in those communities from which likely terrorist recruits are drawn, including the case of 'diaspora' communities (Hoffman, 2007).

Whilst there has been some research on the emotional impacts of counter-terrorism measures on targeted communities (Spalek et al. 2009), rarely have emotions been explored in relation to any engagement and partnerships that may take place between state and non-state actors. As highlighted in the previous chapter, engagement and partnership work are key aspects of counter-terrorism, and this chapter will demonstrate that engagement and partnership between state and non-state actors involve emotional dynamics. As discussed in chapter 4, citizenship is an important aspect of counter-terrorism, with the responsibilisation of particular communities. This chapter will highlight that citizenship is experienced not only legally, politically and socially, but also it is experienced at a profoundly emotional level.

Essentially, counter-terrorism is a field of policy and practice rife with emotions. Being aware of emotions, being able to negotiate these, being able to draw on emotions constructively rather than destructively, these are strategies that practitioners, community members and policy makers should understand and be able to employ to create opportunities for effective work. This chapter provides some analysis and exploration of the role of emotions in counter-terrorism, explaining why emotions should be of concern to practitioners, community members, policy makers and others who work in this field. Data taken from interviews with community members and police officers is presented in order to illustrate the emotional aspects of counter-terrorism. It shows that destructive emotions can be generated by terrorism and counter-terrorism, nonetheless, community members and police practitioners can understand these emotional dynamics at play in order to reduce the harms caused by negative emotions. Community members and police officers can also work towards creating opportunities for the expression of constructive emotions. 'Emotional intelligence' is a theme that is also discussed in this chapter. What does it mean to be emotionally intelligent and why should this matter to practitioners, community members and policy makers when thinking about counter-terrorism as conflict transformation?

Setting the scene: Emotions, terrorism and counter-terrorism

The intangibility and central importance of emotion in understanding socialities renders it complex and challenging to study. Traditionally, emotions have been marginalised by social scientists and by policy makers. According to Walklate (2003), scientific knowledge is that which is dispassionate and impartial, so researchers have rarely studied emotions in any depth, either in relation to the participants in their research or in relation to themselves. Nonetheless, increasingly, emotions have generated more attention. Some feminist researchers consider emotionality to be a central part of documenting and examining the nature of the researcher's subjectivity (see Pickering, 2001). Traditionally, this form of introspection has not been pursued, amid concerns that researchers who explore their feelings might attract accusations of 'unhealthy absorption' or 'emotional exhibitionism' (Pickering, 2001: 486). Nonetheless, this work suggests that by analysing emotionality, there is the potential to reveal hidden decision-making processes that can be linked to power hierarchies inherent in research (Pickering, 2001).

Emotions might be viewed as being active stances towards the world, as well as being responses to situations (Riis and Woodhead 2009:1). Williams and Bendelow (1998: xvi) define emotion as 'existentially embodied modes of being which involve an active engagement with the world and an intimate connection with both culture and self'. They argue that not only do emotions reflect individual experience, but that they also point to the reproduction of wider social structures. For Hochschild (1998), people draw upon an 'emotional dictionary' in order to articulate their feelings, this dictionary being culture-dependent:

> Each culture has its unique emotional dictionary, which defines what is and isn't, and its emotional bible, which defines what one should and should not feel in a given context. As aspects of 'civilising' culture they determine the predisposition with which we greet an emotional experience. They shape the predispositions with which we interact with ourselves over time. Some feelings in the ongoing stream of emotional life we acknowledge, welcome, foster. Others we grudgingly acknowledge and still others the culture invites us to deny completely. (Hochschild, 1998: 7)

Some attention has been paid to distinguishing between constructive and destructive emotions. For the Dalai Lama, much human suffering comes from destructive emotions, for these can breed violence (Goleman, 2003). For Goleman (2003: 53), 'destructive emotions are those emotions that are harmful to oneself or others'. Goleman suggests (2003: 119) that destructive emotions might be viewed as those that are 'byproducts of something useful in human behaviour that in themselves serve no survival function and, in fact, at times have negative survival value'. These include craving, anger, fear, sadness, envy and jealousy. The notion of grievance, so often featured in national counter-terrorism policies, includes space for emotions in relation to feelings of resentment or injustice. Thus, according the Collins Dictionary (2012), grievance is:

a real or imaginary wrong causing resentment and regarded as grounds for complaint
a feeling of resentment or injustice at having been unfairly treated

According to Wright-Neville and Smith (2009), leaders of global neo-jihadist groups draw on emotion to mobilise their audiences into political action. Emotive writing is used, alongside pictures, in order to depict Muslims as victims of mistreatment or humiliation, to try to provoke or escalate anger and outrage within wider Muslim communities.

Terrorists are appealing to wider group collective identities in order to generate a sense of grievance and victimhood (Silk, 2009). It may be that neo-jihadists are seeking to generate powerful emotions associated with an oppressed Ummah (Schmid, 2006). Revenge is being sought for the oppression of Muslims and the emotions being exploited are humiliation, alongside empathy and altruism (Schmid, 2006). It seems important, therefore, to consider the role of emotions in terrorist violence, and particularly for Wright-Neville and Smith (2009) it is the emotions of frustration, anger and humiliation that help drive a person towards incrementally embracing violence, thus:

> ... global terrorist networks such as al Qaeda have entered the emotional marketplace. Their skill lies in an ability to tap into emotions such as anger, frustration and humiliation through a narrative that explains these existential phenomena in terms of victimhood and oppression by outsiders. However, at the same time the narratives pushed by neojihadist groups are designed to stimulate positive emotions such as love, compassion, loyalty, solidarity and pride and then to channel these feelings towards political action. (Wright-Neville and Smith, 2009: 87)

If emotions are viewed as comprised of active stances towards the world, as well as responses to it (Riis and Woodhead, 2009), then terrorists might be viewed as being driven by their emotions as well as their emotions helping to construct their political and violent actions. Those contemporary, as well as historical, events and social contexts which are viewed as oppressive and even cruel can generate the emotional energy that terrorists can draw on to engage in violent action. Contemporary global dynamics mean that individuals can become more aware and sensitive of events taking place from outside of their own locales, so that individuals and the communities that they belong to can become politically inspired to work globally against the policies of nation-state governments. It is important to consider the emotional consequences of colonisation and domination, which have helped to create and sustain many destructive emotions across a wide range of populations, and to note that not all destructive emotions lead to political agency expressed through violence. Non-violent forms of political agency are also plausible responses to destructive emotions (Wright-Neville and Smith, 2009). It should be noted that researchers examining terrorism can also experience a range of emotions – for example, fear (Kleinman and Copp, 1993).

If, as highlighted above, emotions seem to play a role in explaining some instances of terrorism, this raises a number of questions for counter-terrorism policy and practice. For example, how can counter-terrorism initiatives channel destructive emotions into creating forms of political agency that exclude all forms of violence? Similarly, can counter-terrorism initiatives effectively challenge those destructive emotions experienced by individuals who are deemed at risk of committing acts of terrorism, so that they replace their destructive emotions with constructive ones? Should the focus of counter-terrorism measures be implementing far-reaching societal changes that mean that destructive emotions are much less likely to be generated within society? Can structural, cultural and direct violence be abolished without including a focus upon emotions? Interview data with community members involved in counter-terrorism initiatives suggest a number of important ways in which emotions are central for countering violent extremism. A common theme emerging from the research data is that of the role that grievances play in generating destructive emotions that can lead to violent radicalisation. For example, the following is a quotation taken from an interview with a Muslim community member:

> Because those people who get brainwashed into this whole thing are vast majority of the times, don't have any knowledge about Islam. And they've been played upon by the emotions so they come in, someone may come in and say about Palestine or about Iraq or about Afghanistan or about Kashmir, what about this? What about this? And as a result you emotionally get along with it and you think, know what? Maybe he's right. And as a result you end up going down the ... but you yourself must have that knowledge.

The next quotation comes from an interview with a Muslim community member who mentors individuals deemed at risk of violent extremism. Mentoring in relation to violent extremism consists of both a befriending and an interventionist approach, providing a safe space for individuals deemed at risk of extreme violence to discuss issues, and to build a relationship with their mentors (Spalek and Davies, 2012). The mentor below illustrates how extremists attempt to manipulate people emotionally:

> Yeah, towards violence and also as well towards … they manipulate people, get them to try and make them … or example, they'll show you, in those days it used to be John Major, and they used to say that John Major was seen going into a synagogue with a cap on so John Major's a Jew. And for a person who is not really into politics he gets quickly the impression, 'Oh yeah, he's a Jew. So that means he must be helping the State of Israel. Then it means this and then it means this.' And then from then, 'Oh that's why they don't like Muslims. That's why they're bringing in this law,' and, 'That's why they're bringing in that law.' … And I think the main thing through all this is certain texts of our Holy Book, which they use and on the face of those texts they really do think they have a point of what they're trying to say. But it's not until you actually delve into the meaning of how that was applied by our Prophet during his life that you see that it's not necessarily the case of how they try and interpret it.

The quotation below further helps to develop the theme of how important it is for counter-terrorism to understand emotions. It is taken from an interview with a Muslim community member who also mentors those individuals deemed at risk of extreme violence. In the interview the person speaks about building emotionally resilient communities, and the role of theology in helping to do this:

> Promoting the desire to build resilience emotionally and in communities yes, to build more resilient individuals in communities who would be resilient to the threat from terrorism basically … There is a bit of theology so actually I don't have to retract what I've said, I give him some serious moral theological lessons to say remember, anger always responds loudest but silence is a great gift and patience my friend.

The next two quotations come from interviews with two individuals who mentor people deemed at risk of far right extreme violence. In the first quotation, the anger within far rights extremists is highlighted:

But I've spoken to some really quite hot-headed individuals over the years. That's why it made me laugh when sometimes when people say, 'Doesn't it worry you that you speak to these individuals and they can do something to you or physically hurt you or something?' And sometimes you sit and think to yourself, I've never thought of it that way ... Yeah, often they're angry.

In the second quotation below, anger also is highlighted as a key emotion in far right extremists, and how the anger drives a person to look to blame somebody else for how they feel:

A lot of anger, but different emotions. I mean one guy he'd lost his job and he'd blamed the Polish. But we explained somebody Polish, for instance, can't come into this country and say oh, X, I'm having your job. There's reasons why Polish people are given jobs. And that's either because they're willing to take a lower wage, or you might not be working as hard, so they'll get rid of you and give somebody else a job, it's not the Polish person's fault. We explain that but these guys still say we don't give a shit, we still hate Polish. They don't care what explanations we have, it's got that deep rooted now.

In the quotation below this individual who mentors far right extremists explains that racism is not necessarily limited to 'far right extremists' but rather is present within all communities:

In some areas, depending on minority community where they're from, they're the new kids on the block. And historically black families, they were the new communities and they got battered and picked on. And Asian families got battered and picked on. Where now there's some communities where you've got, especially in schools, you've got white kids, black kids, Asian, Pakistani, Bangladeshi, all different kids together who will pick on Eastern Europeans because they're the new minority. So you've got a community that's accepting each other but the new minority, it's gone full circle.

The following quotation taken from an interview with a Muslim community member is interesting because he explains how fear is an emotion that he has experienced when challenging the things that individuals who belong to extremist organisations are saying:

for example, like Hizb ut-Tahrir or one of the other prominent organisations had done, and he'd openly speak about it actually in the lecture. And many times he'd say it and they'd also be sitting there as well, the individuals who were part of the organisations, and then you used to see the questioning and the response live. And by seeing that, I guess that really built me confidence because, for example, sometimes you have a fear, don't you, that when you're going to challenge somebody maybe they might come with an answer which you might not necessarily be able to answer. … And when I used to see that a lot of them, they were just full of hot air and when it come to the crunch of replying back to religious issues that there was nothing really there. I think that really built my confidence, that did.

The above quotation suggests that in order for people to challenge extreme ideologies from within their communities it is important for them to have the confidence to do so. And when they do challenge these ideologies they come to see that there is nothing beyond the rhetoric, no substance.

Emotions clearly are a focus for community-based approaches to counter-terrorism, as illustrated by the quotations above. Powerful, negative, emotions can lead to violent behaviour and so it is important that counter-terrorism initiatives not only focus on socio-structural changes in society, but also on healing destructive, painful, emotions – as Mindell (1995: 19) argues, 'structural work is only a bandage unless feelings have been healed'. Interestingly, within conflict resolution literature, whilst the concept of peace is often discussed and analysed, the related concept of healing rarely features. Healing is a more interesting notion because this refers to the processes of change at individual, community, societal and international levels. Whereas peace suggests an end-goal, healing is suggestive of continuity, of a continual process – for what is the end result of healing and how do we know we have been healed ? Conflicts often lead to substantial traumas, and trauma creates its own conflict, whether at the level of the individual, community, society or internationally. So whilst trauma can undergo healing, it is unclear whether that healing has an end process, an end process that the notion of peace is more suggestive of. Healing also encapsulates the role of emotional as well as psychological, cultural and structural processes. The next section focuses upon the role of emotions in relation to police and community engagement with respect to counter-terrorism. It is suggested that for too long, emotional processes have been excluded from research, policy and practice in this field, and yet data that is presented in this section would suggest that police officers and community members not only engage with political processes but also that they can engage with emotional processes.

Police and community engagement in counter-terrorism and emotions

Mindell (1995: 18) raises an interesting question when he writes that 'there is more to democracy than awareness and the courage when necessary to sit in the fire. But few of us are willing to pay even this minimum price. Who likes to deal with anger and threats?' This quotation applies well when thinking about encounters that take place between state and non-state actors. There is a small body of literature that seems to suggest that whilst state actors are often able to remain dispassionate, embodying the detached 'truths' so highly valued in western thinking, non-state actors, when making claims to 'truth', can be emotionally highly charged. In order to convey their experiences, non-state actors can draw upon graphic and distressing language in order to highlight their suffering. This can be dismissed by state actors who may view such language as being emotionally unbalanced and therefore 'biased' (Spalek, 2008). For example, Puwar (2000) suggests that senior civil servants are represented as the pinnacle of rationalism and impartiality and that this often has racist undertones, with Black individuals being seen as lying outside the (white) norm. With respect to policing, detached rationality is generally valued, whereby 'neutrality, objectivity and impartiality are viewed as necessary antecedents in policing' (Drodge and Murphy, 2002: 425). However, this can create tensions for police officers because not only is police work itself often emotional, but also because policing cultures and rules are affect laden:

> police organizations and police work are affect laden because of cultural and social rules and because of the nature of the work itself, particularly as it occurs at the interface with public law and order (Drodge and Murphy, 2002: 421)

As highlighted in chapter 5, a report by the think tank Demos has emphasised that police officers need to engage much more with political processes and should not view this as compromising their policing roles. Engaging more explicitly with political processes means shaping explicit priorities and allowing other organisations and the public to achieve these (Edwards, 2006). However, in the focus on political processes, emotions have been overlooked. The notion that police officers can be activists who engage with political processes without giving due consideration to emotional processes and their own emotional intelligence is questionable. Indeed, emotions pervade the criminal justice system, for criminal justice can involve responding to the harms that have been perpetrated against victims, their families and wider society. Mindell highlights the importance of reading the emotons of individuals, groups, cities, organisations and the environment, thus:

> the atmosphere of a group – its humidity, dryness, tensions and storms. This atmosphere, or 'field', permeates us as individuals and spans entire groups, cities, organisations and the environment. The field can be felt; it is hostile or loving, repressed or fluid. It consists not only of such overt, visible, tangible structures as meeting agendas, party platforms and rational debate but also hidden, invisible, intangible emotional processes such as jealousy, prejudice, hurt and anger. (Mindell, 1995: 19)

It is important to stress that working with political processes and allowing other organisations and the public to achieve negotiated priorities necessarily involves police officers working with emotional dynamics. Individuals, groups, organisations and even countries (see Moisi, 2009) have emotional landscapes that need to be understood, at least partially, and also negotiated.

Policing responses can themselves generate significant destructive emotions within communities – rage, anger, fear and so forth. These emotions can have historical as well as contemporary dynamics. In relation to counter-terrorism, data taken from interviews with members of Muslim communities suggests that counter-terrorism measures have generated fear in Muslim communities in particular. The following quotation is from an interview with a Muslim woman who talks about fear and anger and the impacts of these emotions on her own engagement with wider society:

> I think the whole criminal justice the way things have gone, detentions, anti terrorism, I think it's you know, it's costing more on civil liberties and things like that and human rights, so it seems too far, I think many people feel very frightened, afraid. You know, for young people, for their sons and younger brothers, and it's creating an atmosphere. I'm not happy at all the way we sometimes, I don't know whether it comes officially or unofficially, the police and the media work hand in hand sometimes, it seems to me to signify the

community as a whole ... It makes me feel angry and just more disinclined to, to be involved and engage, because I feel that it's just the whole thing that's against us.

The following quotation comes from an interview with another Muslim woman who speaks about the impacts of counter-terrorism on the families of those who have been imprisoned for terrorism, and how families can be shunned by their own communities out of fear:

In our area we've got an English Muslim woman who's married to a Dutch man who was recently jailed on terrorism, she's been shunned by the community, she's you know very isolated, she's got four kids ... People are quite difficult to her, people who knew her, used to be friends with her and her husband, they don't want to go to her anymore, visit her anymore, because they're frightened that they will be you know picked on or that they will be associated with her husband's activities. He was found guilty of a relatively minor thing, he was sentenced recently.

The next quotation, from an interview with another Muslim woman, illustrates the fear that people have of counter-terrorism policing:

I would say what the key issue that a lot of people talk about is that they have fear that the police can come into their house at anytime, you know, they have no right and destroy their lives, innocent people ... It's the fear. People genuinely have a fear. There's a fear in the community and they'll just keep quiet, just keep your head down, you know, amongst people who are, you know, families who have, trying to look after their kids and everything. Nobody feels that they have a right to say anything.

Overly hard counter-terrorism measures can create such fear that non-violent political action and debate is repressed, as the following quotation from an interview with a Muslim man illustrates:

There was a leaflet there, this leaflet was about Gaza, what's going on in Gaza. They said 'oh sorry bro, this is just an Islamic stand, like talking about Islam stand' and so they were very afraid of having anything political at university. But this is very scary you know. Because just from the one I was talking to there, they were very worried if they have that literature there that's going to basically affect that university. So this is the climate that's occurred now with either extremism on campus and brothers at university being taken away etc, the people now are afraid to talk about politics.

Communities themselves have complex emotional landscapes with inter- and intra-group dynamics and tensions further adding to the complexities. The following quotation from an interview with a male Muslim illustrates the fear that Muslim communities can experience in going about their daily lives as a result of the media focus on them, and the impacts of this upon police–community engagement:

> Simply because let's say prayers are eight o'clock at night or nine o'clock at night so maybe it's not safe enough to, you know, because maybe there's someone out there walking out of a pub or maybe has just come across the latest headline in the News of the World or the Sun and they see these mosques, they see these people coming out and maybe they want to do something about it. So people are genuinely afraid. ... so I mean you have these layers of fear, of historical kind concepts, the prejudices, you add them all together and it becomes very, very difficult, very, very difficult to build that kind of relationship that you really need in a society such as ours, at times such as ours ... you know, between police and the community.

Effective police practitioners need to be aware of how their own actions may help to generate or awaken destructive emotions, or the ways in which their actions can generate or awaken constructive emotions. Constructive emotions are those considered to be wholesome, positive, and these can include self-confidence, conscience and non hatred (Goleman, 2003). The following quotation, from an interview with a Muslim man, illustrates the fear generated in people as a result of police raids on a particular community in Birmingham:

> The Birmingham raids were, they were frightening raids for a lot of people because the West Midlands police, from what they tell us, they didn't know what was happening. except in the night when they had their ... had a phone call that the counter terrorism unit and Scotland Yard is coming up with their own officers to raid houses ... so all of a sudden we had 700 or 800 officers ... I think there was 700 or 800 officers for those six, seven raids. ... they blocked off all areas, you know, traffic jams the morning, which was chaos that morning, I remember I was coming to work and it was just chaos ... it took me a good part of the morning to find out what actually happened ... I said to one of the officers look you don't need 700 officers to raid seven houses, you know, and blocking off all the areas, you know, and causing traffic jams, kids can't go to school that way, they had to go another way. There were so many things. You just extra frightened the community more than anything else ... they said that

because they came from New Scotland Yard, the terrorism branch, they hadn't had any involvement in it whatsoever.

Emotions can be frightening for people to deal with. Psychodynamic work illustrates the wide range of defence mechanisms that individuals can draw on in order to protect themselves from experiencing uncomfortable or distressing emotions (Freud, 1936). Defence mechanisms include rationalisation, denial, projection. It may be that organisations have their own set of defence mechanisms in order to try to deny the importance and centrality of emotions. Bureaucracy may be one such defence mechanism, for this enables the distancing from emotions through recourse to officialdom and regulations. Police officers can themselves experience many uncomfortable emotions from communities' often emotional demands for information or resources. The following is a quotation from a Muslim man who talks about how police officers may feel:

> and at the same time the police also feel afraid, also feel intimidated, and also feel they are under obligation because in a way they are damned if they do, and they are damned if they don't.

A bureaucratic response that involves drawing on regulatory discourse may be one defence mechanism that some police officers or police bodies use, as this enables them to distance themselves from community actors. Interestingly, a bureaucratic approach to policing characterised by emotional distance can hinder police and community engagement, for community members may feel that their emotions are not being taken on board by police officers and this may add further to a sense of grievance. Tensions are created when individuals attempt to be emotionally distant in highly emotionally charged contexts. The following quotation from an interview with a Muslim male illustrates the tensions created by a bureaucratic policing response:

> It's a two-edge sword really because the police expect us to behave as sensible citizens and respond to their kind of bureaucratic approach. Well look it's all under some committee and it's all being reviewed by an internal body, so we will be dealing with it, but that is just bureaucracy. You are up against bureaucrats who don't really care about us and are not willing to have any emotional involvement in our religion or in our community affairs and that sort of thing and a little bit of progress perhaps but I don't think I can think of anything much that they do offer us you know.

The same person talks about the importance of emotions:

> Well life being as it is, emotions are important, more so than we would perhaps want to recognise. You need when you are dealing with communities, to try to measure and quantify the emotional impact and it's sometimes very very serious and it's never taken into account because police officers are very practical people who deal with practicalities all the time and are not willing or perhaps even able to get involved in emotional concepts. They see it as feminine. But it's one of man's major elements in his intellect, to use and we always do take account of emotion whether we know it or not. It's subconscious you know.

Initiatives that help to generate empathy between police officers and community members can be an important way of building trust. Empathy has to be two-way, and it is as important for police officers to understand the emotional landscapes of the communities with and in which they are working as it is for community members to understand the emotional landscapes of policing cultures, organisations and of police officers themselves (Spalek, El-Awa and McDonald, 2009).

The foregoing discussion should not suggest that a lack of attention to emotions is prevalent within all policing cultures and organisations, nor in all police officers. There are police officers and community members who do work with emotional dynamics, drawing on what might be called their 'emotional intelligence'. In these cases, an acknowledgement and awareness of emotions is used as a way of helping to build effective partnerships grounded in empathy, reciprocity and emotional connections between partners. Emotional intelligence can therefore be used by state and non-state actors in order to build relationships and even partnerships (Spalek et al., 2009; Lambert, 2011). The following quotation from an interview with a Muslim man shows that some police officers can understand and engage with emotion:

> Perhaps police officers have to have a certain coldness and distance to do their work, but the more enlightened ones, going back to X, they seem to be able to understand emotions.

Community members and police officers can perhaps get to know and understand each others' experiences and emotions, for this can help in building empathy between them, which is an important aspect of building trust (Booth and Wheeler, 2007). It also can be the case that community members and police officers can share emotional experiences as a result of interconnected experiences and their multiple identities. So, for example, since 9/11 Muslim police officers may share the distrust and fear that many Muslim community members may experience as a result of the politicised environment in which Islam has come under increased political scrutiny. Muslim police officers may also experience similar fears and anxieties as Muslim community members about any backlash they may experience from their wider communities as a result of being involved in counter-terrorism work (Spalek, 2010). Emotions can therefore be shared through shared identities and shared social experiences, and this applies as much to police officers as to other people. Police officers are not immune to emotions, and are not wholly 'outsiders', rather, they too are affect-laden entities who may draw upon their emotions in order to build empathy and bridges with the communities that they help police.

Conclusion

This chapter demonstrates the importance of a focus on emotions for counter-terrorism policy and practice. It seems that terrorists can generate destructive emotions in individuals who are susceptible to their messages and this in turn can lead to further violent action. It seems that terrorists appeal to wider group collective identities in order to generate a sense of grievance and victimhood. Destructive emotions are those that are harmful to oneself or others, and they include anger, fear, sadness, envy and jealousy. This chapter presents data gathered through interviews with community members and police officers engaged in counter-terrorism work. The data presented here in relation to the role of emotions in counter-terrorism raises a number of important issues. It seems that overly hard counter-terrorism measures can create such fear in specific communities that non-violent political action and debate is repressed; this can potentially and inadvertently lead to violent political action. Effective community-based approaches to counter-terrorism seem to involve community members being aware of, and working with, emotions, and transforming destructive emotions into constructive ones, which might be viewed as those that are wholesome and positive, and can include self-confidence, conscience and nonhatred.

This chapter also gives some focus to counter-terrorism policing in relation to emotions. Whilst policing organisations may value detached rationality, this can create tensions for police officers because not only is police work itself often emotional, but also because policing cultures and rules are affect laden. At the same time, communities themselves have complex emotional landscapes with inter and intra group dynamics and tensions further adding to the complexities. The notion that police officers can engage with political processes without giving due consideration to emotional processes and their own emotional intelligence is questionable. Policing responses can themselves generate significant destructive emotions within communities – rage, anger, fear and so forth. A bureaucratic approach to policing characterised by emotional distance can hinder police and community engagement, for community members may feel that their emotions are not being taken on board by police officers and this may add further to a sense of grievance. Tensions are created when individuals attempt to be emotionally distant within highly emotionally charged contexts. This chapter suggests that effective police practitioners need to be aware of how their own actions may help to generate or awaken destructive emotions, or the ways in which their actions can generate or awaken constructive emotions. It is also important to note that community members and police officers can share emotional experiences as a result of their interconnected experiences and their multiple identities. This chapter serves to highlight that counter-terrorism involves emotional work, and that the transformation of destructive emotions into positive ones, and the generation of constructive emotions, should be a key focus for policy makers, practitioners and community members. A focus upon emotions, therefore, is another aspect to viewing counter-terrorism as conflict transformation. The next chapter takes the key theme of counter-terrorism as conflict transformation and examines this through questions of governance.

Bibliography

Booth, K. and Wheeler, N. (2007) *The Security Dilemma: Fear, Cooperation and Trust in Politics*. Palgrave Macmillan.

Collins Dictionary (2012) http://www.collinsdictionary.com/dictionary/english/grievance (accessed 2 May 2012).

Drodge, E. and Murphy, S. (2002) 'Interrogating Emotions in Police Leadership' *Human Resource Development Review* Vol. 1, 420–38.

Edwards, C. (2006) 'The Activist Police Force' in J. Craig (ed.) *The Everyday Encounters of Citizens and Professionals should help them to build Autonomy* London: DEMOS, pp. 52–60.

Freud, A. (1936) *The Ego and the Mechanisms of Defence*. New York: Karnac Books.

Goleman, D. (2003) *Destructive Emotions and How We Can Overcome Them*. London: Bloomsbury.

Hochschild, A. (1998) 'The Sociology of Emotion as a Way of Seeing' in S. Williams and G. Bendelow (eds) *Emotions in Social Life*. London: Routledge, pp. 3–15.

Hoffman, B. (2007) *The Radicalization of Diasporas and Terrorism*. A joint conference by the RAND Corporation and the Center for Security Studies, ETH Zurich: Rand Corporation.

Hülsse, R. and Spencer, A. (2008) 'The Metaphor of Terror: Terrorism Studies and the Constructivist Turn' *Security Dialogue*, 39(6), 571–92.

Kleinman, S. and Copp, M. (1993) *Emotions and Fieldwork*. Newbury Park, CA: Sage.

Lambert, R. (2011) *Countering Al-Qaeda in London: Police and Muslims in Partnership*. London: Hurst and Company.

Mindell, A. (1995) Sitting in the Fire: Large Group Transformation Using Conflict and Diversity. Oregon: Lao Tse Press.

Moisi, D. (2009) The Geopolitics of Emotion: How Cultures of Fear, Humiliation, and Hope are Reshaping the World. New York: Anchor Books.

Pickering, S. (2001) 'Undermining the sanitized account; violence and emotionality in the field in Northern Ireland'. *British Journal of Criminology* Vol. 41, pp. 485–501.

Puwar, N. (2000) 'The racialised somatic norm and the senior Civil Service', *Sociology*, vol 35, no 3, pp. 351–70.

Riis, O. and Woodhead, L. (2009) *A Sociology of Religious Emotion*. Oxford: Oxford University Press.

Schmid, A. (2006) 'Magnitudes and focus of terrorist victimization', in U. Ewald and K. Turkovic (eds) Large-scale Victimisation as a Potential Source of Terrorist Activities: Importance of Regaining Security in Post-conflict Societies. Amsterdam: IOS Press.

Silk, D. (2009) 'Outreach between Muslim Communities and Police in the UK: Preliminary Report', https://getd.libs.uga.edu/pdfs/silk_phillip_d_201005_phd/silk_phillip_d_201005_phd.pdf (accessed 3 April 2013).

Silke, A. (2001) 'The devil you know: continuing problems with research on terrorism', *Terrorism and Political Violence*, 13(4), 1–14.

Spalek, B. (2010) 'Community Policing, Trust and Muslim Communities in Relation to 'New Terrorism'. *Politics and Policy*, Vol. 38 (4), pp. 789–815.

Spalek, B. and Davies, L. (2012) 'Mentoring in relation to Violent Extremism: a study of role, purpose and outcomes' Conflict and Terrorism Studies 35:5, 354–68.

Spalek, B., El-Awa, S. and McDonald, L. Z. (2009) 'Engagement and Partnership Work in a Counter-Terrorism Context'. Birmingham: University of Birmingham.

Toros, H. (2008) 'Terrorists, Scholars and Ordinary People: Confronting Terrorism Studies with Field Experiences', *Critical Studies on Terrorism*, 1(2), 279–92.

Walklate, S. (2003) 'Can there be a Feminist Victimology?' in P. Davies, P. Francis and V. Jupp (eds) *Victimisation: Theory, Research and Policy* Basingstoke: Palgrave Macmillan, pp. 28–45.

Williams, S. and Bendelow, G. (1998) *The Lived Body: Sociological Themes, Embodied Issues.* London: Routledge.

Wright-Neville, D. and Smith, D. (2009) 'Political rage: terrorism and the politics of emotion' *Global Change, Peace and Security*, 21:1, pp. 85–98.

7

Governing Terror; 'Top-down' and 'Bottom-up' Approaches to Counter-Terrorism

Introduction

The introduction of community-based approaches to counter-terrorism raises a number of important issues around questions of governance. Traditionally, covert counter-terrorism approaches have consisted of 'top-down', state-driven structures of accountability. Covert approaches have not necessarily been subject to significant public scrutiny, even when such approaches have been controversial with there being a fine line toed between legal and illegal activities. Community-based approaches to counter-terrorism will involve community members, non-state actors who themselves will bring a level of public scrutiny to this arena. The involvement of community members in counter-terrorism raises a number of issues around governance in relation to questions of 'bottom-up' approaches to counter-terrorism; community cohesion and freedoms associated with liberal democracy; and risk. This chapter focuses on these key issues in order to discuss the implications of community-based approaches for counter-terrorism. This chapter highlights that after 9/11 the 'War on Terror' involved a top-down approach to security which was linked to geo-political power plays between nation-states in relation to world order. The 'War on Terror' is thus a politicised global strategy, helping to re-configure security issues at the level of the nation-state and the locale, impacting upon Muslim communities in particular. At the same time, after 9/11 'bottom-up' approaches to counter-terrorism were also instigated, which involved engagement and even partnerships between communities and state actors and agencies. Underpinning both 'top-down' and 'bottom-up' approaches are tensions between responses that emphasise community cohesion, and those that emphasise liberal freedoms associated with liberal democracy. The former can problematise Muslim identities as a whole, whilst the latter do not necessarily view religious, political or other identities as problematic. It is preventing violence that is the focus of policy and practice. This chapter discusses these tensions and their implications for community-based approaches to counter-terrorism. Quotations from community members, police officers and others are also provided in this chapter in order to illustrate more fully some of the points made.

Governance and counter-terrorism

To govern is to influence or determine, whereas governance is the actual act or manner of governing. According to Brennan et al. (2007: 13), 'the world of governing has seen a revolution expressed in a shift from government to governance'. For Brennan et al. (2007), the notion of governance is to be understood as that which includes both government and civil society, with the state and civil society engaging in decision-making and other processes, through the interaction of top-down, state-led, imperatives and bottom-up approaches which include networks, groups, communities and others that are part of what might be deemed civil society. It would appear that the notion of governance is key in exploring and understanding community-based approaches to counter-terrorism.

In relation to counter-terrorism, governance might be viewed as comprising two inter-related, and at times conflicting, dynamics. On the one hand there are 'top-down' global and nation state approaches to counter-terrorism, and on the other hand there are 'bottom-up' approaches that involve state and non-state actors implementing mostly localised approaches. 'Top-down' approaches comprise geo-political power plays between countries which can significantly influence the security policies of nation-states. In relation to Al Qaeda-linked terrorism, responses have been dominated by a 'War on Terror' that was initially instigated by the administration led by former US President Bush. The 'War on Terror' might be viewed from the perspective of global governance as being top-down, comprising dominant political and economic actors and authorities determining the legitimacy of risk in relation to questions of security, being linked to wider geo-political power plays between nation states in relation to the global world order (Findlay, 2007). The 'War on Terror' might thus be thought of as a politicised global strategy, helping to re-configure security issues at the level of the nation-state and the locale. Through the hegemonic project of globalisation there is a quest for community at a global level, a war on pluralism and the construction of a 'war on terror' which has served to target and alienate those communities viewed as being opposed to western modernisation (Findlay, 2007). 'Top down' governance approaches therefore include international and nation state-led approaches that prioritise the maintenance of a global world order and nation state security over individual and community security concerns.

'Bottom-up' approaches to counter-terrorism are those that stress community involvement, in which partnerships and engagement between communities and state agencies is influenced by the concerns and experiences of those communities. The involvement of communities in relation to countering threats from 'new terrorism' reflects theit involvement in tackling other problems such as anti-social behaviour, unemployment and so forth. The governance of 'new terrorism' reflects broader developments in governance, whereby responsibility and accountability for preventing terror crime, as with traditional forms of crime, is increasingly focused towards local levels, whilst still maintaining centralised control in terms of resources and target setting. Also, formal responsibilities for policy implementation and service delivery are progressively being shared across statutory and voluntary agencies and community groups in the form of partnership work. A further aspect to the governance of 'new terrorism' which might be linked to bottom-up approaches is reflectivity. Here, the greater visibility of security intelligence in the public domain has led to an increased awareness, scrutiny and critique by politicians, media commentators, NGOs, communities and the general public.

It is important to note that community forums can be important mechanisms through which to hold police to account. Forums that involve police and community members engaging with each other can be challenging. For example, a study by Spalek et al. (2009) examining police and community engagement, highlights that the diversity of the Muslim population poses significant challenges for engagement. It may be that some groups place higher value on organising demonstrations and vociferously expressing their concerns to the police, whereas other groups prefer an approach that involves implicitly expressing their concerns whilst maintaining good relationships with police. These different viewpoints and styles of engagement inevitably lead to tensions between groups and individuals. The Muslim Safety Forum (MSF) is a forum that was set up in 2001 and made up of a wide range of Muslim community organisations, including the Muslim Council of Britain (MCB), the Islamic Human Rights Commission (IHRC), the Islamic Forum Europe (IFE) and other organisations. The MSF held regular meetings at Scotland Yard with senior police officers from the Metropolitan Police Service, to discuss community safety, policing and counter-terrorism issues. It is important to stress that community forums can be challenging for their participants because there can be a wide range of views about how to hold police officers to account and how to engage with them. The quotation below from a Muslim police officer illustrates the diverse voices on the MSF and the challenges for their oversight of the police:

> ... let's say for example you had the X, they had their own remit and good luck to them, they had their own focus you know, and there's a particular way in which they like to do business. Then you have Y which has their own way of doing business, you know their own version of diplomacy and the fact that they would seen to be meeting people like the Prime Minister and their secretary would be seen to be meeting with senior cabinet people etc., etc. It's very unlikely that you're going to get people from X having that kind of a cordial relationship, because they have a different way of working ... So they had different approaches so therefore, when they come into the Muslim Safety Forum, they're sitting round the same table talking, each one brings their own perspective okay. So there was difference of opinion around that table.

In some cases it is difficult for particular communities to be engaged, as the following quotation from an interview with a police officer illustrates:

> There are groups that are particularly difficult to engage with, such as youth groups, um, and certainly newly arrived communities. Some communities will have baggage either from, quite rightly, from the police in London or somewhere 20, 25 years ago or ten years ago or five years ago or whatever it is. Others will bring baggage from if they come from outside the UK, sometimes they'll have a cultural issue in dealing with the police that, that is a barrier. Um,

and all you can do is just be around, speak to them, try and bring them along, engage with them, drip by drip by drip. But it's an ongoing process and one of development.

Moreover, it is important for individuals who participate in forums to be doing so on behalf of their communities rather than for their own personal or political interests, as the following quotation from an interview taken with a police officer highlights:

> … big challenge is getting a, a really committed community representative and somebody who's not, you know, participating for their own personal or political ends. Erm, and it comes with some sensitivity as well because if you're in any way exposing them to the individual cases they would have to be fully vetted, you know, because there's a degree of information sharing.

According to Spalek, Beleza, Limbada and McDonald (2012), community members who are participating in forums or other mechanisms of engagement with police, often have to grapple with the following concerns:

> I want to work in partnership with organisations such as the police, local authority or named person as I want to protect my community …
> I want to have an input at the table as I am a community representative/leader …
> I do not want to accept any Prevent related funding, but I may interact with counter-terrorism officers …
> Do I trust the police and do I have confidence in how they work?
> Are the police targeting Muslim communities due to the high number of stop and searches and the high level of terrorist arrests impacting on this group?
> How do I ensure the police remain accountable to the community?
> Are the police only interested in policing the political and religious thoughts of a particular ethnic/religious group? What about the threat from the far right?
> How do I test the notion of partnership working and accountability?
> By cooperating with counter-terrorism police, will I be perceived as a "sell out" to my community?

Bottom-up approaches are therefore complex, and providing community oversight of counter-terrorism is, similar to other areas, challenging.

It is important to stress that top down and bottom up approaches to counter-terrorism involve both state and non-state actors, in that both state and non-state actors can be part of global, national, top-down approaches as well as being part of bottom-up and reflective governance approaches. Indeed, the idea that communities can defeat terrorism features in both top-down and bottom-up approaches, with the notion of 'community' predominantly viewed through the lens of 'problem' within top-down approaches whilst in bottom-up approaches community is viewed largely as 'solution'. There may also be significant tensions between top-down and bottom-up approaches. For example, bottom-up approaches may involve partnership work between state agencies and those communities deemed 'suspect' by global and nation state top-down approaches. Therefore, state actors involved in engaging and developing long-term partnerships with members of 'suspect' communities are likely to attract criticism, not only from top-down perspectives but also from the wider public domain where dominant discourses like the 'War on Terror' have gained hegemony. Lowndes and Thorp (2010: 123–4) stress that 'tensions between a locally driven, community-focussed approach and a nationally led, security-oriented agenda have been ongoing'. It is important to elaborate further on what some of these tensions are, between 'top-down' and 'bottom-up' approaches to the governance of counter-terrorism. The research that I and my team have been involved in suggests that, in particular, there are tensions between approaches that emphasise community cohesion, and those that emphasise liberal freedoms associated with liberal democracy. The former can problematise Muslim identities as a whole, for Islamic ideology here is portrayed as dangerous and in conflict with 'western values' (Jackson, 2005) and so Muslims are viewed as not integrating with wider British society. The latter do not view religious, political or other identities as problematic, only largely preventing violence is viewed as the focus of policy and practice. There also can be tensions over risk: who identifies risk, how this is managed and ultimately who decides whether a set of vulnerabilities constitutes risk of violent extremism.

Security as community cohesion and/or as liberal freedom?

Community cohesion in relation to terrorism has featured significantly in public policy debates. According to the Cantle Report on community cohesion (2001), ignorance about each others' communities can easily grow into fear, especially where this is exploited by extremist groups determined to undermine community harmony and foster divisions. The report's authors further observed that although the physical segregation of housing estates and inner cities came as no surprise, they had been repeatedly struck by the degree to which the existence of 'separate educational arrangements, community and voluntary bodies, employment, places of worship, language, social and cultural networks, means that many communities operate on the basis of a series of parallel lives'. For authors of the Cantle report, there needs to be a greater collective and individual effort for all sections of the community to improve their knowledge and understanding of each other, also for the largely non-white community to develop a greater acceptance of, and engagement with, the principal national institutions.

Interestingly, research suggests that higher levels of community cohesion might be linked to lower crime rates. According to Wedlock (2006), cohesive communities have the following characteristics: a sense of community, similar life opportunities, a respect for diversity, political trust and a sense of belonging. According to Wedlock (2006), local areas with a high sense of community, political trust and sense of belonging show significantly lower levels of 'all' reported crime. Sampson and Groves (1989) found that community cohesion was directly linked to a reduction in mugging, street crime and stranger violence. More recently, Sampson and Raudenbush (1999) have found that social control takes the form of people in cohesive neighbourhoods being prepared to pull together and intervene in deviant or criminal activities for the public good. They defined this type of collective efficacy as 'cohesion amongst residents combined with shared expectations for the social control of public space'. They found that collective efficacy is associated with lower rates of crime and social disorder even after controlling for structural characteristics of the neighbourhood. Wedlock (2006) points to other research that suggests that the links between cohesive communities and reduced crime are not only a British and American phenomenon. Lee (2000) used data from 15 countries in the 1992 wave of the International Victimisation Survey in order to provide an international comparison of the role that community cohesion plays in reducing the risk of individual violent victimisation. He found that the higher levels of social control or guardianship apparent in a cohesive community reduce the likelihood of becoming a victim of violent crime such as robbery and assault, regardless of socioeconomic status, lifestyle and neighbourhood characteristics.

In debates about the risks for terrorism that a lack of community cohesion and integration can pose it is Muslim communities that have featured predominantly in relation to counter-terrorism policy. Some have suggested that Islam as a religion is in a state of flux, with political and ideological conflict taking place similar to the struggles in Christianity during the Reformation (Modood, 2007). According to Modood (2007: 23), 'the upheavals and wars that characterise the Reformation are present in the Muslim world today but non-Muslim powers, especially the US, are major players'. Post 7/7, minorities are expected to conform to and assimilate the dominant norms of British society, culturally and religiously. It has therefore become commonplace to construct certain Muslim practices and beliefs not only as markers of difference, but as barriers to 'positive community relations', as illustrated by Jack Straw's comments[1] – as a public servant – on women's face coverings as a 'visible statement of separation and of difference'. 'Muslim difference' has been viewed as dangerous, and a dichotomy now exists between 'moderate' and 'radical' Muslims. Narratives found previously in American neo-conservative commentaries, such as the RAND Corporation's testimony 'Moderate and Radical Islam' (Rabasa, 2005) have become mainstreamed into British government counter-terrorism strategy (Spalek and McDonald, 2010). Any groups deemed 'radical' are, if not constructed as potential violent actors, categorised as creating an environment in which terrorist activity may be inspired or flourish. Therefore, Muslim who appear to value the Ummah over feelings of Britishness, or to isolate themselves from wider society, are negatively judged and seen as a threat to social cohesion. Within government rhetoric, those Muslims and community organisations that are viewed as being 'moderate' are seen to be allies in the prevention of terrorism (Spalek and Imtoual, 2007). It seems that all kinds of value judgements have been placed onto Muslim communities, distinguishing between legitimate and illegitimate Muslim identities. Legitimate Muslims are perceived to be those who engage with governments on the terms set by those governments. Those Muslims who refuse such an engagement (irrespective of their motivations or reasons)

[1]   http://www.guardian.co.uk/commentisfree/2006/oct/06/politics.uk (accessed 30 January 2012)

are likely to be perceived as 'radical' and hence a potential terrorist threat. This creates an untenable situation for many Muslims (Spalek and Imtoual, 2007). Spalek and Lambert (2008) have argued that wider questions about community and social cohesion should not define the terms of engagement with Muslim communities for the purposes of counter-terrorism. Rather, a rational assessment should be made, according to which groups can best help combat extremism, and questions of cohesion and national identity should be left to other fields of policy-making. Although research has highlighted that engaging marginal and marginalised Muslim groups such as 'Salafis' and 'Islamists' is a logical continuum of the post 7/7 drive to support community-led, faith-based approaches to youth work, education and de-radicalisation central to the Prevent agenda (Lambert, 2008; Spalek et al., 2009; Baker, 2011), this is problematic in terms of government policy, as government policy focuses on the notion of 'shared values' within CONTEST 2, the Brritish government's main counter-terrorism stratgey. According to CONTEST 2 (Home Office, 2009: 13):

> we will take action against those who defend terrorism and violent extremism. We will also continue to challenge views which fall short of supporting violence and are within the law, but which reject and undermine our shared values and jeopardise community cohesion. Some of these views can create a climate in which people may be drawn into violent activity ...

Problematically, the above paragraph – reflected in later sections in the document (ibid, 87) – lacks crucial precision: terms such as terrorism, extremism, shared values and community cohesion are diffuse and contested notions, open to a high degree of interpretation. This is perhaps unsurprising: as argued elsewhere, engagement work for the purposes of counter-terrorism is a highly politicised arena in which debates around broader, normative issues in relation to citizenship, multiculturalism and values continue to take place, profoundly influencing engagement work (Spalek and Lambert, 2008). The focus on 'shared values' is problematic because local problems of socio-economic marginalisation and exclusion, and related inter- and intra-community tensions within ethnically and religiously diverse British cities are conflated with the globally constructed social problem of 'new terrorism'.

There can therefore be significant tensions between approaches to counter-terrorism that emphasise community cohesion, and those that emphasise liberal freedoms associated with liberal democracy. As discussed above, the former can problematise Muslim identities as a whole, for Islamic ideology here is portrayed as dangerous and in conflict with 'western values' (Jackson, 2005), so Muslims are viewed as not integrating with wider British society. At the same time, particular political, religious and ethnic identities, associated with being a Muslim and with a perceived increased risk of committing acts of violence, are securitised. Approaches that emphasise liberal freedoms seek not to problematise or securitise particular identities, but rather to enable individuals to draw upon the liberal freedoms associated with liberal democracy. Thus a wider range of actions are considered legitimate, so that individuals do not see violence as a means to pursue their aims. This work includes a wide range of activities such as encouraging political participation from within Muslim communities, enhancing education about Islam among Muslims themselves, and supporting social and political activism. This work also seeks to draw upon individuals formerly and/or currently practising 'securitised identities' as mentors in order to attempt to rehabilitate those deemed at risk of committing acts of violence, so that they are no longer at risk from pursuing violent action.

As highlighted in chapter 2, embedding Muslim youth who are at risk of becoming violently extremist within those communities that are likely to carry greatest legitimacy with them might prevent their drift towards violence as a means of action. This work, however, is under constant threat of being criticised by a fear-fuelled media and political frenzy, which views the empowerment of communities or groups that are seen as 'fundamentalist' or 'separatist' as serving to feed Islamic extremism. A more rational viewpoint might be that working in partnership with minority Muslim groups may constitute part of a broader, multicultural dynamic. For, in the process of engagement work, both state institutions and Muslim communities are involved in mutual interaction and dialogue, within which there are of course points of contestation. Ongoing engagement work might be seen as constituting part of a pluralistic process whereby community groups can help to shape government policies and the practices of state agencies, as well as being themselves shaped by these (see Modood, 2007). Ongoing engagement work might be viewed as influencing the very cultures of those groups involved in partnership. Therefore, an aspect of partnership work may be that those groups involved in engagement are reciprocally influencing each other's cultures, where cultures are seen as constructed by 'crossover', by hybridization and by innovation' (Young, 1999: 89). Drawing upon the work of Castells, it may be that 'bottom-up' approaches to counter-terrorism involve a process through which identities can be shaped. Individuals holding resistance identities, which are those generated by individuals who occupy devalued or stigmatised positions within society, who may build resistance due to feeling different from, or being opposed to, principles permeating the institutions of society (Castells, 2004), can, through effective counter-terrorism practice, be inspired to become project identities. Project identities seek to transform society through political and social action. Project identities can even eventually become dominant in the institutions of society, thus becoming legitimising identities. Counter-terrorism practices can thus shape resistance identities and empower them to become project and even legitimising identities through a focus on political and social agency which excludes violence. This approach is vastly different from an approach in which particular identities are problematised. In relation to AQ-linked terrorism, Islamist and Salafi communities have in particular been problematised by counter-terrorism policies because Islamism and Salafism have been viewed as posing a subversive threat to Europe (Spalek and Lambert, 2008). Lambert (2008) has argued that a broad alliance of powerful and influential politicians and commentators are adamant that the AQ terrorist threat is just the tip of an Islamist–Salafi iceberg. As such police should be encouraged to target and monitor Islamists and Salafis as subversive groups or organisations rather than seek to serve them as minority communities. Therefore, it follows that to empower Islamists and Salafis is to legitimise and appease subversives and extremists. However, the research by Lambert (2008), Spalek et al. (2009), Baker (2012) and others challenges this viewpoint through stressing that engagement and partnerships with Islamist and Salafi groups is not only desirable but essential to reducing AQ-linked terrorism in Europe, the US and other areas. Here, religion, politics, Muslim identities and practices are embraced rather than viewed as dangerous or antithetical to social cohesion. Community members are encouraged to co-operate with the police on what is viewed as a common aim, the protection of society at large from crime committed in the name of Islam (Spalek et al. 2009). What is apparent, therefore, is that law enforcement agencies are operating within a conflicting counter-terrorism environment. On the one hand, where social and community cohesion is stressed then 'hard' policing tactics are encouraged in order to flush out potential 'subversives'. On the other hand, where liberal freedoms within democracies are emphasised then 'softer' counter-terrorism tactics involving engagement and partnerships are pursued. Future research could therefore examine the tensions and overlaps between these different styles of law-enforcement approaches as part of a wider exploration of the complex refashioning of identity and affiliation within the 'new age of terror' in relation to sovereignty, 'extreme' identities, counter-subversion and counter-terrorism (Spalek and McDonald, 2011). Importantly, the tensions between 'hard' and 'soft' policing approaches can also be played out by those police officers working in counter-terrorism themselves. The quotation below comes from an interview with a Muslim police officer who was being asked to work for an overt counter-terrorism policing unit:

> So there is that uncertainty, then there is uncertainty in the counter-terrorist remit, what's that involve? If it means that you are going to be picking up a phone or something and listening to a conversation, of course, we don't do that, that's something else, but if it meant that you have to do that, what would I do under those circumstances, would I turn around and tell them I'm Muslim, sorry, I'm not doing that? Would I face discipline, would I not face discipline, they're all unanswered questions and uncertainty as to what that work involved, okay.

The same officer speaks about needing reassurances from his police seniors, as he did not want to be involved in any covert policing activities that might compromise his relationship with his community:

> And so I wanted some reassurances on wanting to know more about that role and everything because I couldn't, I wouldn't do it, you know, it's for me as a Muslim to go around doing it and to be seen to be spying … it immediately sets off a whole part of your community against you, that trust that you build up over the years as a police officer, who everybody knows is a police officer and to build up that trust and that relationship and, you know, getting them to work, even the kind of people that never ever dreamed about working with the police service; getting them to work with you and subtly, they see you as somebody who's … spying on people or gathering intelligence. It immediately puts you in a

very different light in the eyes of the Muslim community particularly you know. Remember it's difficult for people to talk to the police anyway to report a crime, to be a victim and then to go to the police is very difficult for people, especially in the Asian Community, the immigrant community, the Muslim community, other communities, it's very difficult. Even more difficult for them to come and talk to somebody that they think is an intelligence officer.

Community members can also experience the tensions between being viewed as covert intelligence sources and community partners:

There is always that thought because one of our members was actually approached by MI6 and asked to co-operate as an informer and that was our very own committee members, so if they are approaching our bodies, you know MCB, Muslim Parliament, Welfare House, wherever, you know it means that we may well be a suspect, because they have chosen us to try and recruit us.

In the above quotation, the person highlights how members of Muslim communities have been approached by the security services and have been asked to act as informants. This same community member goes on to explain that community members want to remain independent, and do not want to be seen as spies for the authorities:

But we as a whole don't want to be considered as spies for the authorities, we want to retain an independence from authority and show respect to them and we hope that we receive respect back. The relationships just now are fairly well, but they are extremely difficult at the time of the East End attack on those two brothers that I mentioned to you.

It is also worth drawing attention to the mention that the community member makes regarding hate crimes committed against two Muslims, which placed strain onto relationships between Muslims in the East End of London and the authorities.

Risk

When exploring community-based approaches to counter-terrorism, risk is a key issue. Indeed, most of the chapters in this book include some discussion of risk. In relation to the governance of counter-terrorism, 'bottom-up', community-based approaches raise a number of issues of risk.

The involvement of community members in counter-terrorism initiatives can mean that community members play a crucial role in helping to assess risk. For initiatives that do not problematise 'extreme' identities but rather which work with individuals in order to encourage wide-ranging non-violent political and social actions it can be problematic to judge the extent to which individuals risk committing violence. Such initiatives are often led by community members rather than state actors and so it is community members that can play a significant role in assessing risk of violent extremism, especially as there may be aspects to individuals' lives that only community members can witness and understand. The following quotation is from a community member involved in community-based counter-terrorism initiatives, talking about risk assessment:

> it's a judgement call that you've got to make in terms of what you know of this individual and other factors, in assessing what you believe to be the risk in terms of the behaviour, the activity, or the comments that you hear or see, or that are reported to you. So it was really very much a case of, you know, trying to work out whether is this just a, you know, an individual who is boasting, bragging, seen a programme on TV etc? Or is it actually somebody who is genuinely being groomed, influenced, you know, and that's something that you have to really make that judgement call.

This is why strong partnerships between community members involved in community-based initiatives and police officers are essential, for police officers must be able to trust any risk assessments made by community members. Governance in relation to community-based approaches to counter-terrorism therefore raises the question of who it is that identifies risk; ultimately who decides whether a set of vulnerabilities constitutes risk of violent extremism? There may be a danger of tending to over-assess vulnerability and for too many cases to be brought to the attention of neighbourhood police officers, who then have to decide whether a particular case is so insubstantial that it does not require the attention of counter-terrorism units nor of intervention providers in relation to preventing violent extremism. At the same time, it may be that all cases deemed 'borderline' are passed on to counter-terrorism units or to intervention providers and so there is a potential here for net-widening, for bringing in greater numbers of individuals for intervention. A study by Spalek and McDonald (2011) found that some police officers are adopting a minimalist approach, preferring other agencies and professionals to assess and deal with any dangers posed by individuals displaying inappropriate behaviours, and for police to be brought in when the behaviours and the risks are deemed severe. There is of course another inherent issue here: in encouraging agencies and staff across a wide range of sectors to look for signs of vulnerability in the first place, society is encouraged to look for risks in relation to violent extremism. With the focus of the Prevent strategy having been on Muslim communities there is the inherent danger that Islamic beliefs and practices are stigmatised (Spalek and McDonald, 2010). Our research also raises some deeper questions – in a situation where risk is being assessed by different agencies, whose voice carries most weight? Is there a potential for the voice of the communities to be marginalised? Is there not a very fine line in risk-assessing cases of individuals who might be dealt with constructively under preventative work but who might also be dealt with through an investigative approach? Who ultimately decides whether an individual has passed from being at risk of committing acts of violence to being about to commit them? Moreover, in relation to the notion of partnership, is there equality, transparency and legitimate cooperation between partners when cases that fall between Prevent and Pursue are apparent? At the same time, our interviews suggest that partnerships that are created can sometimes exclude community members from key decisions that are made, with community members having to 'chase up' statutory agencies. When linking this to the notion of risk, the question is raised whether community members can at times be excluded even within engagement that is based on a model of partnership.

'Bottom-up', community-based approaches to counter-terrorism also raise questions over risk in relation to information-sharing protocols. There may be a danger that statutory agencies enter into relationships and agreements with community members that may prioritise the risk and other needs of those agencies rather than the risks and the needs of community members themselves. Community members who work with the police and other agencies as part of multi-agency forums assessing risk may be placing themselves at high risk of reprisals from members of their own communities or any networks to which they belong. Therefore, agreements that fully represent the requirements and operating parameters of both the communities and of the police and other statutory agencies are crucial. It is important to take into consideration, and to acknowledge, that within multi-agency approaches to assessing and working with risks of violent extremism, community members may face risks that statutory agencies do not face, and vice versa, hence the need for clear discussion about how any protocols of engagement can capture the needs of both communities and statutory agencies (see also Baker, 2011).

Community-based approaches can involve overt counter-terrorism police officers working in partnership and engaging with communities. A study by Spalek and McDonald (2011) highlights that sometimes overt counter-terrorism police officers working with communities on the ground may not be given all the information on a particular case from covert policing units, yet may be asked by these units to check out a piece of information with, say, a community member. This requires further exploration: the overt counter-terrorism police officer could be placing themselves at an unknown level of risk, and may not be quite sure why they are being asked to speak with particular community members. It may therefore be that there needs to be further discussion and analysis of the linkages between overt and covert approaches, and the information that is shared between them. Overt counter-terrorism police officers can play an important role in highlighting to covert counter-terrorism units the actual or potential impact of covert or any other policing operations upon communities. Future research needs to explore the extent of any influence that overt approaches are having on covert approaches, to explore the dialogue and interaction between the two in more detail. Thus, in 'bottom-up' community-based approaches to counter-terrorism, professionals and not only community members can also face certain risks themselves. Professionals may engage in actions that they argue helps prevent violent extremism but that the agencies that they work for will perhaps discourage them from undertaking. This may be partly because the organisational cultures of the agencies themselves are more risk averse than are the individuals working for them. One example that might illustrate the point is that of a youth worker who took young, marginalised, disenfran-chised Muslims to a Stop the War march because he thought that this was a positive way for the young people to display their anger at foreign policy. This was also seen as an opportunity for building community cohesion in that the young people noted how many of those on the march were neither Muslim nor from minority ethnic backgrounds but from white communities (Spalek and McDonald, 2011).

It is important to highlight that within community-based approaches to counter-terrorism involving community members and police, both are taking risks. It may be that community members view the police as a 'last resort' in preventing violence, preferring first to challenge appropriately and prevent violence themselves before seeking help from the police. As highlighted in chapter 2, community members cannot be seen to be overtly and repeatedly seeking help from the police as this can undermine their credibility with community members who may be suspicious of police. The following quotation from a Muslim community member serves to illustrate this point:

> it's high risk, that is very, very high risk. There's been incidents where you know if it doesn't go the right way someone's getting killed. There's people armed in front of you. But if you don't deal with it in that way, these individuals, you'll lose their trust, their confidence, and they will go to extremists. (Muslim Community Member [5] 2008) (from Spalek, 2010: 804)

Community-based approaches to counter-terrorism may involve community members also sorting out everyday crime and other related issues themselves, and only seeking direct police action as a last resort. This raises the question of who ultimately has responsibility for policing ? Community members and/or police officers ? Where community members are involved in policing then how is accountability maintained ? The following is a quotation from a Muslim community member who has been involved in policing issues from within his own community:

> An individual turns up in a big mackintosh because he had a dispute with another Muslim and the size of the weapon he had down the back of his coat and what did we do? Did we panic and run and call the police? We took him round the corner, my colleagues, spoke with him, really calmly.
>
> What are you doing? You're coming to a religious place, this is the house of God, it's a mosque. And you're coming to kill a Muslim? Do you know that killing a Muslim means that you go to the hellfire straight away? Eyes wide. Really? So if I killed this individual I will be punished? Yes you will. And even if he was wrong and he do this you'll still do this because you are not an authority to take anybody's life. What did he do? Jumped in the car, went home, put his

weapon away, came back, made up with the individual. (Muslim Community
Member [5] 2008) (in Spalek, 2010: 804)

Community-based approaches to counter-terrorism are likely to be particularly problematic within areas that are experiencing political transitions, where
there may be a 'divided sovereignty'. Findlay (2007) argues that para-politics
operate beyond the reach of conventional state authority and highlights that
these dynamics add further complexity to law-and-order strategies designed
to maintain social order. Within areas marked by conflict and transitions,
there may be no common acceptance of appropriate law-and-order responses,
and so who is responsible for maintaining law and order and how it is
governed are key questions. According to Knox (2001), writing in the context
of Northern Ireland, punishment beatings and shootings are ways in which
paramilitaries have 'policed' their areas. Paramilitaries in Northern Ireland
have claimed that they take action against joyriders, burglars, paedophiles,
car thieves and other types of criminals. Historically, communities have been
discouraged from going to the police. Knox's (2006) study illustrates that
within a zone of conflict, alternative mechanisms for dealing with law and
order exist because state-based organisations may be distrusted. They may
be viewed as being owned by 'the other side' or simply be considered to be
ineffective. But the 'street level' maintenance of order in these contexts is not
to be mistaken for the kind of social control that naturally occurs in cohesive
communities discussed earlier. In this context, order is enforced through
paramilitary groups and militias whose loyalty is to their own groupings
rather than to the community as a whole.

Conclusion

This chapter explores some issues around questions of governance and
community-based approaches to counter-terrorism. The chapter highlights
that there can be tensions between approaches to counter-terrorism
that stress community cohesion and those approaches that stress liberal
freedoms associated with democracy. It points to an unresolved question
for many counter-terrorism practitioners, for policy makers, for researchers
and for community members: within a society, where should the balance

lie between the embracing of ethical freedoms in relation to 'extreme' identities, and the governance of identity? Extreme or radical identifications are not necessarily problematic but violent actions associated with them are. Therefore, can there be alternative forms of agency that allow for the expression of radical or extreme identities that are democratic and do not involve violence? This chapter has shown that the 'War on Terror' associated with AQ-linked 'new terrorism' comprises a set of rationalities and technologies which are top-down, international and national state policies instigated and influenced by elite political, social, media and other groupings. Nonetheless, 'bottom-up' approaches that are community-based can challenge 'top-down' approaches. 'Bottom-up' approaches that stress liberal freedoms can involve working with individuals and groups deemed 'dangerous' by 'top-down' approaches. 'Bottom-up' approaches involve community members and potentially bring greater public scrutiny of counter-terrorism. However, as this chapter also demonstrates, the involvement of community members in engagement and oversight of counter-terrorism can be challenging.

Bibliography

Baker, A. H. (2011) *Extremists in Our Midst* Basingstoke: Palgrave Macmillan.

Brennan, T., John, P. and Stoker, G. (2007) ' Re-Energising Citizenship: What, Why and How?', in T. Brennan, P. John and G. Stoker (eds), *Re- Energising Citizenship: Strategies for Civil Renewal*. Basingstoke: Palgrave Macmillan, pp. 8–25.

Cantle report (2001) *Community Cohesion: a report of the independent review team* Chaired by Ted Cantle Home Office.

Castells, M. (2004) *The power of identity* (2nd edn), Oxford: Blackwell.

Findlay, M. (2007) 'Terrorism and Relative Justice' *Crime Law and Social Change* 47: 57–68.

Home Office (2009) CONTEST: the UK's Strategy for Countering Terrorism London: HMSO, https://www.gov.uk/government/uploads/system/uploads/attachment_data/file/97995/strategy-contest.pdf (accessed 3 April 2013).

Jackson, R. (2005) *Writing the War on Terrorism: Language, Politics and Counter-Terrorism* Manchester: Manchester University Press.

Knox, C. (2001) 'The 'deserving' victims of political violence: 'punishment' attacks in Northern Ireland' *Crime and Criminal Justice* 1 (2) 181–99.

Lambert, R. (2008) 'Empowering Salafis and Islamists against Al-Qaida: A London Counter-Terrorism Case Study', *PS: Political Science and Politics* 41(1): 31–5.

Lee, M. R. (2000) 'Community Cohesion and Violent Predatory Victimization: A Theoretical Extension and Cross-national Test of Opportunity Theory' *Social Forces.* 79 (2): 683–8.

Lowndes, V. and Thorp, L. (2010) 'Preventing Violent Extremism – Why Local Context Matters', in R. Eatwell and M. Goodwin (eds), *The New Extremism in Twenty-First-Century Britain*. London: Routledge, pp. 123–42.

Modood, T. (2007) *Multiculturalism*. Cambridge: Polity Press.

Rabasa, A. (2005) 'Moderate and Radical Islam', CT-251, testimony presented before the House Armed Services Committee Defense Review Terrorism *Counter-Terrorism* and Radical Islam Gap Panel on 3 November 2005, RAND Corporation testimony series, http://www.rand.org/content/dam/rand/pubs/testimonies/2005/RAND_CT251.pdf (accessed 4 December 2011).

Sampson, R. J. and Groves. W. B. (1989) 'Community Structure and Crime: Testing Social-Disorganization Theory' *American Journal of Sociology* 94: 774–802.

Sampson, R. J. and Raudenbush, S. (1999) 'Systematic Social Observation of Public Spaces: A New Look at Disorder in Urban Neighbourhoods' *American Journal of Sociology* 105: 603–51.

Spalek, B., Beleza, R., Limbada, Z., Silk, D. and McDonald, L. Z. (2012) *Impacts of Counter-Terrorism on Communities* Unpublished paper.

Spalek, B., El-Awa, S. and McDonald, L. Z. (2009) 'An Examination of Partnership Approaches to Challenging Religiously-Endorsed Violence involving Muslim Groups and Police' University of Birmingham published report.

Spalek, B. and Imtoual, A. (2007) ' "Hard" Approaches to Community Engagement in the UK and Australia: Muslim communities and counter-terror responses' *Journal of Muslim Minority Affairs*, Vol. 27 (2), pp. 185–202.

Spalek, B. and Lambert, B. (2008) 'Muslim Communities, Counter-terrorism and De-radicalisation: a reflective approach to engagement' *International Journal of Law, Crime and Justice* Vol. 36 (4), pp 257–70.

Spalek, B. and McDonald, L. Z. (2010) 'Anti-Social Behaviour Powers and the Policing of Security' *Social Policy and Society* Vol. 9 (1), pp. 123–33.

—(2011) 'Preventing Religio-Political Violent Extremism Amongst Muslim Youth: a study exploring police-community partnership' University of Birmingham.

Wedlock, E. (2006) 'Community Cohesion and Crime' Home Office Crime and Cohesive Communities Online Report 19/06 Research and Development Directorate.

Young, J. (1999) *The Exclusive Society*. London: Sage.

Conclusion

Engaging Communities for Twenty-First-Century Security

For too long, counter-terrorism practice has carried with it stigma, being associated with infiltration, spying on communities, the implementation and the over-use of state powers against those considered to be 'suspect'. Counter-terrorism is a notion that has gained a certain notoriety, a certain reputation, for being unethical, for involving the violation of human rights, and for being secretive and lacking in public scrutiny and accountability. Steve Hewitt (2010), in his illuminating book called *Snitch!*, demonstrates that informers have been evident for centuries, being essential tools for the state to collect information on its citizens. In the US, for example, during the era of radicalism, the 1960s and 1970s, informers in the Black Power, Red Power, gay and liberation movements were employed by the FBI and CIA to monitor domestic dissent. The Soviet Union, with its secret police, pursued political radicals through the infiltration of secret collaborators, and informers were celebrated as doing their civic duty. It is estimated that under the German Democratic Republic, 2–3 per cent of the population were informers (Hewitt, 2010). More recently, post 9/11, with the US led 'War on Terror', accounts have emerged of Arab and Muslim communities in particular experiencing over-policing. To illustrate this, the following is a quotation taken from a book written by Zighen Aym, an American citizen of Algerian origin, who was asked to come for an interview by the FBI because he had been seen taking photographs of spiders next to a railway track which had aroused the state's suspicions:

> When the formal interview began the first questions focussed on information I knew the FBI already had: Name and address. Like a surgeon's scalpel, the intrusive questions poked me, each cutting deeper and deeper, and the

> dissection, though physically painless was mentally traumatizing. I regretted
> having agreed to the interview, for while I had done nothing wrong, I had to
> divulge both personal and professional information to prove my innocence. I
> felt as if some powerful system had negated the principle 'innocent until proven
> guilty'. (Aym, 2005)

This quotation clearly demonstrates the kind of pain that over-zealous
counter-terrorism practices can create. These kinds of experiences, issues
and debates are ongoing. In Britain, for example, the Channel Project has
generated some criticism. Channel is a controversial national scheme established to support those individuals vulnerable to recruitment by violent
extremists. It uses the resources and experience of professionals who provide
an ongoing support package. Described as a multi-agency process with a
diverse grouping involving police, social services, health, youth offending
team workers and community individuals, the group is mostly chaired
by a local authority employee or a community person with sensitive case
details provided by the police. Whilst some channel panels have community
involvement, issues around security clearance, data protection (around legislative impact), confidentiality and extent of Criminal Records Bureau (CRB)
checks retain police nervousness due to the sensitive casework data of
vulnerable individuals being shared in a non-police domain, even if they are
counter-terrorism partners (Kundnani, 2009). The Channel Project is referred
to in the Prevent Review document 2011, thus:

> In many areas, these programmes are now delivered through Channel, a police-
> coordinated, multi-agency partnership that evaluates referrals of individuals at
> risk of being drawn into terrorism, working alongside safeguarding partner-
> ships and crime reduction panels ... Channel is modelled on other successful
> multi-agency risk management processes such as child protection, domestic
> violence and the management of high risk offenders. It uses processes which
> also safeguard people at risk from crime, drugs or gangs ... the Channel process
> comprises three discreet steps: identification; risk assessment and referral; and
> support. The guidance states that identification of vulnerable people should be
> made by a wide range of statutory organisations. They include local authorities;
> police; youth offending services; social workers; housing and voluntary groups.
> Identifications must be made carefully and against a range of possible indicators
> ... The indicators (if observed) set the bar for referral quite high and would not
> (as is sometimes claimed) enable the referral of people simply for the holding

of political opinions or having commitment to a faith. They include: expressed support for violence and terrorism; possession of violent extremist literature; attempts to access or contribute to violent extremist websites; possession of material regarding weapons and/or explosives; and possession of literature regarding military training, skills and techniques. Under a section entitled 'personal history' the guidance proposes that attention be paid to: claims of involvement in organisations; espousing violent extremist ideology; claims of attendance at training camps; and claims of involvement in combat or violent activity on behalf of violent extremist groups. (Prevent Review, 2011: 60)

Any referrals should be made to a Channel coordinator who then assesses, with senior statutory partners, whether the person who has been identified is vulnerable to terrorism, whether they should exit the programme or whether they should be referred elsewhere (Prevent Review, 2011). According to figures released by the Associations of Chiefs of Police (ACPO), the number of Channel referrals nationally stands at 1120 between April 2007 and the end of December 2010 (ACPO, 2012). According to media reports, by 2009, two hundred schoolchildren in Britain, some as young as 13, were identified as potential terrorists by this scheme, raising concerns that the police run the risk of infringing upon children's privacy (*The Independent*, 2009). In 2011, MPs criticised Channel for triggering accusations about teachers and community leaders being asked to spy on Muslim youths (*The Guardian*, 2011). There is indeed a danger in pursuing an overly zealous counter-terrorism agenda. As much of this book has highlighted, particular communities can become 'suspect' and this raises issues for civil liberties.

The contribution of *Terror Crime Prevention with Communities* is that it attempts to propose ethical ways of doing counter-terrorism practice, at the core of which there lies an understanding that counter-terrorism is really about conflict transformation. Reframing counter-terrorism as conflict transformation helps state and non-state actors to work through their differences, to value each others' differing perspectives and experiences, and to work together in order to reduce the potential for extreme forms of violence. Chapter 2 has clearly illustrated the competing claims to truth evident in a post 9/11 era, and suggests that at the core of counter-terrorism as conflict transformation is the notion of credibility. Credibility is about a person's positionality, how a person draws upon their multiple identities in order to build trust and relationships with key audiences and potential partners. Credibility can be challenging, for it is about being prepared to challenge dominant power structures in order to try to secure social justice, in a world characterised by social injustice. Credibility can play an important transform-ative role within conflict precisely because it is about maintaining integrity and trust despite considerable pressures to conform to dominant norms that may include repression, human rights abuses, violence or the promotion of violence. Credibility can be an important resource through which to build and maintain important connections with a wide range of actors for the purposes of conflict transformation, of offering peaceful responses to social norms and practices that are unjust and even violent.

Chapter 3 has examined community policing in relation to counter-terrorism, an area that has generated substantial research and policy interest. The chapter highlights that there is a danger that community policing is co-opted into state-driven agendas that almost exclusively focus on Muslim communities when responding to terrorism. At the same time, the chapter suggests that there is a danger that community policing might overlook the role of social and political factors in underpinning any community support for terrorism or other forms of extreme violence. This chapter also highlights the importance of police and communities engaging with each at times other than during a crisis event, as this can serve to humanise police and community relations. It is important, though to highlight that there can be important differences in perceptions between police officers and communities. Thus, police officers may express the real need for a covert style of counter-terrorism policing, and that communities cannot expect 'hard' policing tactics to be removed for the sake of relationship-building, even though communities argue that they dislike the use of tactics like surveillance, stop-and-search and informant-based approaches. Chapter 3 is generally supportive of adopting community policing within a counter-terrorism arena, although various limitations and questions must be considered. For example, could the appli-cation of 'softer' skills that feature in more covert, security-service led approaches within overt counter-terrorism policing contexts decrease the legitimacy of the police, particularly when the legitimacy of policing is often based on accountability and the rule of law being seen to be upheld and equal for all citizens?

Chapter 4 has considered how, within a context of differentiated citizenship, where there may be competing loyalties associated experiences of belonging at a global, as well as national and local level, states can encourage and actively persuade citizens to work within state-driven counter-terrorism agendas. The notion of active citizenship – that individuals as citizens have a responsibility to help prevent terrorism – that is at the heart of 'softer', community-based strategies to counter-terrorism, is highlighted. However, although citizenship at an abstract level implies equality, in reality individuals experience different levels of citizenship. When looking at citizenship in relation to nation-state security, particular communities have experienced differentiated state-led approaches to counter-terrorism. Post 9/11, Muslim communities have particularly experienced differentiated citizenship because they have borne the brunt of 'hard-edged' counter-terrorism policies and practices that have included detention without charge, surveillance and the use of informants. Therefore the chapter asks whether members of Muslim communities can take a proactive civil stance towards national counter-terrorism strategies and work towards preventing terrorism. Or, is it the case that the focus for all active citizens, not only for Muslims, should be a critique of state-driven counter-terrorism policies and practices where, despite state rhetoric around communities defeating terrorism and enhancing community resilience, in reality counter-terrorism continues to be largely driven by 'hard-edged' approaches that include surveillance and infiltration? A key theme highlighted in chapter 4 is that of trust. It seems that trust enables state and non-state actors to negotiate spaces of engagement and even partnership within the complex counter-terrorism terrain. This suggests that underpinning 'softer' counter-terrorism policies and practices are themes that resonate more directly with conflict transformation – the ability of state and non-state actors to work through any struggles and incompatibilities they may have, with trust serving as the social glue for this.

Chapter 5 has focussed on engagement and partnership within a counter-terrorism context. Key themes highlighted include: the importance of general engagement with a wide range of community members; the importance and challenges of engaging and partnering non-violent radicals; how engagement and partnership can involve several different meanings and approaches relating to enhancing the quality of life for communities, building inclusivity, developing connections with women, building relationships, engaging with wider political issues, moving at the community's pace, respect and understanding; how there can be tensions between 'hard-ended' intelligence-led approaches to counter-terrorism, in which community engagement and partnership are not priorities, and 'softer' community-focused approaches that are about relationship-building; and how information sharing is a key issue for engagement and partnerships.

Chapter 6 looks at the role of emotions in counter-terrorism practice. It seems that terrorists can generate destructive emotions in individuals who are susceptible to their messages and this in turn can lead to further violent action. Chapter 6 has suggested that destructive emotions are those that are harmful to oneself or others, and they include anger, fear, sadness, envy and jealousy. Overly hard counter-terrorism measures can create fear in specific communities that non-violent political action and debate is repressed and this may potentially and inadvertently lead to violent political action. Effective counter-terrorism practice involves state and non-state actors being aware of, and working with, emotions. Effective community-based approaches to counter-terrorism seem to involve transforming destructive emotions into constructive ones, which might be viewed as being those that are wholesome and positive, and can include self-confidence, conscience and nonhatred. This chapter also gives some focus to counter-terrorism policing in relation to emotions. Whilst policing organisations may value detached rationality, this can create tensions for police officers because not only is police work itself often emotional, but also because policing cultures and rules are affect laden. At the same time, communities themselves have complex emotional landscapes with inter- and intra-group dynamics and tensions further adding to the complexities. The notion that police officers can engage with political processes without giving due consideration to emotional processes and their own emotional intelligence is questioned in chapter 6. Policing responses can themselves generate significant destructive emotions within communities – rage, anger, fear and so forth. A bureaucratic approach to policing characterised by emotional distance can hinder police and community engagement, for community members may feel that their emotions are not being taken on board by police officers and this may add further to a sense of grievance. Tensions are created when individuals attempt to be emotionally distant within highly emotionally charged contexts. Chapter 6 suggests that effective police practitioners need to be aware of how their own actions may help to generate or awaken destructive emotions, or the ways in which their actions can generate or awaken constructive emotions.

Chapter 7 has explored questions of governance and community-based approaches to counter-terrorism. The chapter looks at 'top-down' and 'bottom-up' approaches to counter-terrorism. It is argued that underpinning both 'top-down' and 'bottom-up' approaches are tensions between responses that emphasise community cohesion, and those that emphasise liberal freedoms associated with liberal democracy. The former can problematise specific identities, whilst the latter do not necessarily view religious, political or other identities as problematic. It is preventing violence that is the focus of policy and practice. The chapter points to an unresolved question for many counter-terrorism practitioners, for policy makers, for researchers and for community members: within a society, where should the balance lie between the embracing of ethical freedoms in relation to 'extreme' identities, and the governance of identity? Extreme or radical identifications are not necessarily problematic but violent actions associated with them are. Therefore, can there be alternative forms of agency that allow for the expression of radical or extreme identities which are democratic and do not involve violence ?

A core theme underpinning *Terror Crime Prevention with Communities* is that counter-terrorism practice is dominated by 'top-down' state-led approaches to security. *Terror Crime Prevention with Communities* is an attempt to strengthen, support and further establish an evidence base for 'softer' community-based approaches to counter-terrorism. Whilst community-based work within counter-terrorism is complex and fraught with difficulties, the book presents data about how state and non state actors have negotiated the multiple and multi-layered challenges. Implicit within *Terror Crime Prevention with Communities* is the idea that despite 'new terrorism' discourse resulting in a reduction of civil liberties, particularly for members of Muslim minorities, community-based work can help to re-set the balance. As such, community-based work can be part of a broader strategy of empowerment and transformation for twenty-first century peace-building. Importantly, *Terror Crime Prevention with Communities* has presented empirical data illustrating vastly different experiences and perceptions of counter-terrorism practice. Trying to link these different narratives together to present a coherent framework of analysis is perhaps impossible. This is an important point, given that due to the politicised arena of counter-terrorism, often dominant elites decide on a particular set of policies and practices and then fit research and empirical data around these in order to validate their particular approaches and rationales. What happens if the approach taken to the analysis of empirical data contains elements of grounded theory, whereby themes are allowed to emerge from the data itself rather than being guided by particular political or policy frameworks and outcomes ? A grounded theory approach is one that my research team and I have undertaken, and one which underpins *Terror Crime Prevention with Communities*. This has generated fragments of experiences and perceptions about community policing, counter-terrorism, police and community engagement, trust, emotions and other themes. These fragments are real-world, human experiences, and as such are invaluable. It is important to stress that the data presented in this book has not been tampered with in order to promote a particular philosophy, ideology or political standpoint. As highlighted previously, counter-terrorism policy and practice contains struggles over 'truth'. As such, counter-terrorism as conflict transformation involves the production of data that is not politically or ideologically motivated. Only then is it possible to create approaches that are for the betterment of all citizens, rather than approaches that are under-pinned by political posturing and defensiveness. *Terror Crime Prevention with Communities* is an attempt to sow some seeds of ethical counter-terrorism practice, through a lens that views counter-terrorism as a form of conflict transformation. *Terror Crime Prevention with Communities* bears witness to the many practitioners, community members, policy officials and researchers who have shown significant leadership and courage in implementing ethically-driven initiatives aimed at preventing terrorism. The debates and issues presented in *Terror Crime Prevention with Communities* are likely to resonate for many years to come.

Bibliography

ACPO (2012) National Channel Referral Figures, http://www.acpo.police.uk/
ACPOBusinessAreas/PREVENT/NationalChannelReferralFigures.aspx. (accessed
17 August 2012).

Aym, Z. (2005) *Still Moments: A Story About Faded Sreams and Forbidden Pictures.*
Mossville: Still Moments.

Home Office (2011) Prevent Strategy London: HMSO, https://www.gov.uk/
government/uploads/system/uploads/attachment_data/file/97976/prevent-
strategy-review.pdf (accessed 10 April 2013).

Hewitt, S. (2010) *Snitch! A History of the Modern Intelligence Informer.* London:
Continuum.

Hughes, M. (2009) 'Police identify 200 children as potential terrorists'. *The
Independent,* 29 March 2009, http://www.independent.co.uk/news/uk/crime/
police-identify-200-children-as-potential-terrorists-1656027.html (accessed 17
August 2012).

Kundnani, A. (2009) *Spooked! How not to prevent violent extremism.* London:
Institute of Race Relations.

Travis, A. (2011) 'Schools' counter terrorism project reviewed'. *The Guardian,* 18
February 2011, http://www.guardian.co.uk/politics/2011/feb/18/schools-counter-
terrorism-project-review (accessed 17 August 2012).

Index

CPSIA information can be obtained
at www.ICGtesting.com
Printed in the USA
LVOW01s1705270716

498006LV00005B/130/P